WHEN THE CURTAIN FALLS

"Exposing the Dark Side of Blue"

REDINA THORPE THOMAS

DEDICATION

This book is dedicated to the memory of my mother, Barbara Jean Wiggins Thorpe McKiver. She was a rare gem who took her rest on March 1, 2020. I also dedicate this book to my brother, Robert Leonard Thorpe, who preceded her in death on July 31, 2010.

I am honored to dedicate my first solo project to the remembrance of my momma who was the woman God chose to give me life and foster my gifts and talents. Thank you, Momma, for giving me life and teaching me by example how to be a woman of valor. I thank you, Heavenly Father, for choosing my momma to guide me. She was a strong and selfless woman who loved her family and fought for my voice when I didn't know I had a voice worth fighting for. I am thankful for the way she battled for my life when I was too afraid to do so. Thank you for believing in me and understanding the great seed God allowed you to birth. Thanks to you and God, my greatness has been re-birthed. To my brother Robert, you were my first sibling protector and my inseparable love. We were two peas in a pod and when our roles were reversed,

I did what a sister should do to be there for you. I helped build you back up so God could show his glory through you, and I watched you be restored in God's eyes and become an angel amongst us. Just as in Exodus 12:2-3, "on the 10th day of the first month, a lamb was to be chosen for Passover". God chose you and Momma to be the sacrificial lambs so I could carry the mantle and be all God created me to be. Because of your love and support, our family was spared from attacks against us; just like the Israelites were spared from the plague of death.

ACKNOWLEDGEMENTS

I acknowledge my daughters, Tre'Nese and Telicia Thomas, and Tenia Thomas-Hines, whom I love dearly and who have supported me through many trials. I appreciate them for supporting me in my dreams, and for loving me despite my failures and imperfections. My father, Robert Lee Thorpe, Jr., for affording me a sound educational foundation through his outstanding hard work ethic. Bonus Father, Luther Lasarus McKiver, for being an amazing grandfather, bonus dad, and spiritual leader of our family. My brother, Roderick, and sister, Shannon Thorpe, for being a support system as I raised my daughters and for stepping in to assist me whenever needed. My aunts, uncles, and cousins who have always been in my corner waiting for me to step out in faith. You know I have mad love for you! My nieces and nephews, who love me for just being their Auntie Dina. Laurentina Bryan Wingster, my beloved sister who has been there when no one else was there providing me with comfort, love, and guidance through the pain and hurt as I navigated my way. Pastor Alan Dwayne O'Neal, a friend and my Pastor, who has stirred my gifts and poured into me. Pastor Frank Ellis, Jr., who has helped by supporting me through the trials of the loss of my mother. Principal/Alderwoman/Interim Superintendent, the late Gwendolyn Goodman – for always encouraging me, leading me to victory and caring for my daughters. Thank you to the late Dr. Prince Jackson, who knew me as a little girl and served as a positive role model and mentor. He was instrumental in my success as a former director of *Pathways to Teaching*. Dr. Evelyn Dandy, who gave me a fresh start at *Armstrong Atlantic State University* as a student-teacher supervisor who imparted great knowledge and professional guidance. Margaret Ilugbo Hunter for staying up with me many nights guiding me as I wrote countless papers. My publisher, Joan T. Randall, for her support and encouragement during the writing process. Last but not least, Cheryl Polote-Williamson for presenting me with an opportunity to begin to share my pain and helping me begin the healing process. Thank you for being a true sister and showing me how to not only dream again, but how to turn those dreams into reality.

TABLE OF CONTENTS

FOREWORD

When Redina first told me about *When the Curtain Falls,* I was instantly elated because I knew just how much I could have benefited from her story. She was a co-author in one of my previously written books, so I know how her story will help countless others rediscover peace and be empowered to chase each one of their dreams. Reflecting on my earlier years, I can recall mistakes I made and how many of them could have been avoided had I been given the right advice from the onset. With the courage exhibited in writing this book, there will be a lot of insightful advice given through the testament of her story which is geared to help you, as the reader, live a fulfilling life full of love and happiness.

My friendship with Redina has transformed into sisterhood since growing up together in Savannah, GA, and her presence in my life has become nothing short of invaluable. To date, we still talk about how it was growing up together compared to where we are now. I am proud of our growth mentally and spiritually. We are always quick to give advice and support each other in many decisions, and most importantly, we challenge each other to continue to grow and develop into a better version of ourselves.

In this book, you will learn who you let into your personal space and who you keep out of your personal space is a key factor in finding clarity and focus as you become your best self. Redina has refused to allow me to settle in *any* area of my life, and I love her dearly for it. She has always helped me remember I must embrace happiness and my passions, dismissing any negativity from those who would like me to believe my ever-evolving goals are unachievable.

Redina is always there not only to celebrate my success but to lend a helping hand when I stumble and I will always do the same for her. After over 40 years of friendship, I am happy and honored to write this foreword for *When the Curtain Falls*. Redina is unconditional in both the love and the support that she exhibits, and I am confident that it will be evident as you read her amazing story. There are not many people who I call "sister," but Redina is one of the best. I am excited for each of you to learn how everything that happened behind the curtain helped her to develop into the phenomenal woman she is today. I truly hope you enjoy this book.

For the love of happiness and freedom,

Cheryl Polote-Williamson

Best Selling Author, Life Coach & Global Media Executive

INTRODUCTION

Since 2017, several people across the country have taken note of my story in a book entitled *Soul Source*, where I shared a glimpse of the domestic violence I faced throughout my marriage. Many women and men of God prophesied to me how important it was for me to write my own book and give life to my story. It was time for me to trust my gifts and God-given talents and share them with the world. I want to be who God says I am; living a life of truth and transparency and free of man's judgment in every area of my life. This book exposes "me" and all I have done while in the world. God washed me whiter than snow and His words are mine to own. He wants to grant me the desires of my heart, so here I am! There comes a time in life when you must be accountable for your mistakes, even though they may not be pretty. Those mistakes may look like an old dry rotted curtain, but God will refurbish and revitalized that curtain into something so beautiful that it is unrecognizable. As we open the curtain, the light peeks through because we have told the truth. What was meant to destroy us and our families did not prosper and, by God's grace, we have weathered the storms and are still standing tall. I

3

hesitated sharing my entire story for fear of human judgement, but later decided to fear God's judgement instead.

The purpose of a rod is to suspend curtains, usually above a window or alongside one to enhance the ambience of the environment. My life was much like drapery — just there for decoration. The fabric looked good from the outside but needed to be cleaned up internally. As Mehmet Murat Ildan once said, "Instead of hiding behind the curtain, be the curtain itself; you will never be found," because looks can be deceiving. The time has come for me to live a life of total transparency and release the good, the bad, and the ugly. I had to figure out how to clean my life up after domestic violence, molestation, rape, a failing career, betrayal, grief, unforgiveness, and a lack of balance. I said I wanted to walk with Jesus, I received my marching orders and I am taking the first step. In order for me to experience the power in movement, I had to first let the curtain fall. I remember lying in my bed about a year ago when God gave me the title of my book, *When the Curtain Falls.* "That's the one!" I gleefully proclaimed. I jumped up and down with joy after receiving confirmation, but the work was just beginning. When it is time for the proverbial curtain to fall, you will experience a lot of different emotions happening simultaneously. You may be startled that the curtain fell, or you may be upset because now you must fix it. You may not really want to put in the work to put the curtain back up, so you may contemplate whether or not you should just leave it down. You may realize the curtain was not straight and when you try to re-hang and align it, it may still fall back down if not properly supported. My life has been much like that of a curtain. Up today and down tomorrow. I wanted to be fortified and balanced, similar to a curtain relying on the support structure provided by a curtain rod. I wanted my life to sit straight on the windowsill. Unfortunately, my life was much like an ornate curtain looking good on the outside, but needing to be cleaned up. There were a lot of curtains across the room that needed to fall before this transition could take place. It is my prayer you will receive a glimpse into my life and how I navigated through the betrayal, relationships, stress, career, ministry, and unforgiveness I faced while finding balance and preparing for a new love.

WHEN THE CURTAIN FALLS

❧

"Exposing the Dark Side of Blue"

Blue has always been a beautiful color to me, as it represents the beauty in the sky and the peacefulness of the passionate waves of the sea. It represents the attributes of trust, loyalty, confidence, faith, stability, intelligence, heaven, and many of the qualities one would look for in a "soul mate". Blue can also represent depression and the dark depths of the human psyche.

During the latter part of 1993, I met a police officer, Mr. Blue, who was working off-duty at the grocery store I frequented. I usually had three or four girls with me when I visited the store, and he would walk with us down the aisles as I shopped. His attention flattered me, and I was appreciative of any help he offered, but I was not romantically interested in him. What I perceived as a kind man providing a watchful eye over me and my girls turned out to be a predator prowling for something far greater than shoplifters.

One day my cousin stopped by the store and saw him talking to me. As she walked back to her car, she yelled to me across the

7

parking lot he was a nice guy and I should give him a chance. I typically wouldn't date any man without getting a good reference on him. I tried to date decent men, but my past decisions proved my power of discernment was ineffective. The words "power of discernment" can be a melodious tone in one's ears, especially for a young naïve mother of three.

One evening as I was leaving the store, Mr. Blue casually slipped his number in my hand after helping me load my groceries into my car. "Call me sometimes," he said while gazing into my eyes. "I want to take you to see a movie." My adrenaline was pumping, but even though I kept his number, I was not planning on calling him. I was dating an up-and-coming attorney, Mr. Noble, at the time who had made it clear he would never marry a woman with three small children. He enjoyed me as his playground, but after nearly a year had passed, I realized my relationship with Mr. Noble had run its course so I gave Mr. Blue a call. I am a huge Whitney Houston fan, so when he invited me to see the movie The Bodyguard on the big screen, I was excited.

The date seemed somewhat awkward. On the way to the movies, he placed his feet on the dashboard of my car and would say things like "Don't be using big words on me — talk to me so I can understand you." There were other things that made me uncomfortable, like his constant drinking, but at the time I didn't have a heightened awareness of spiritual discernment. There is a still, quiet voice that alerts us to signs of potential distress, but at the time I was not equipped to fight off the devil's tactics. I was in the world and of the world and despite the subtle warning signs, what I thought was love resulted in my children being scarred.

While attending a birthday party for one of my daughter's friends, the adults were in the front yard enjoying themselves as the children played with road bikes. My youngest daughter was about to step one foot off the curb to get off of her bicycle when I observed a car swerving in her direction with the music blasting. The driver was flirting with a female passenger and did not see or hear me yelling at the top of my lungs for him to stop. I saw my daughter's life flash right before my eyes as the car hit her, causing her to flip in the air three times. I thought her head was going to be crushed under the tire of the car, but by God's grace, it wasn't. Crying hysterically, I dialed 911 and then called my younger brother, who was furious when he arrived at the scene of the accident. He acted rather aggressively towards the young driver and had to be calmed down or face being arrested. I rode in the ambulance and comforted my daughter as she headed to the hospital to be treated for her traumatic injuries.

I waited until I left the hospital to notify her father, my ex-husband, Mr. Cain and when he heard about what happened, he became very upset and blamed me for not properly watching his children. His temperament was far from mild and very unpredictable, and I lived in constant fear whenever he would come around. When he arrived at my momma's house later that evening, a disturbance ensued as he aggressively threatened me and my brothers who were there to defend my honor. They had grown weary of the disrespect that Mr. Cain exhibited toward me, especially in our Momma's home, no less!!

While the police were approaching the house, they saw my brother kick Mr. Cain's truck and perceived my brother to be the aggressor. While I was trying to explain to the officer that there was an active warrant against Mr. Cain because of domestic violence charges, my brother refused to calm down, so the policeman attempted to arrest him. While the officer struggled on the ground trying to arrest my brother, a button on his walkie-talkie was pressed and alerted the entire police force that an officer was in need of help. That sent an entire fleet of patrol cars to my momma's home. After a long night of explanations and pleading from my momma, I was grateful that the police officers did not take my brother to jail that night. As I thanked and hugged one of the policemen, I noticed that one of the other officers was Mr. Blue.

A few days later, Mr. Blue knocked on my door to check on me and my daughters. It was not a simple task raising three daughters alone, and I always felt something critical was missing in my life — a father for my daughters. I was subconsciously trying to fill the role of a father in their life because of Mr. Cain's infrequent visits and long absences from their life. He was never there to assist me with parental responsibilities, and even though he was granted liberal visitation rights, he never exercised them. I was uncomfortable with our arrangement because I knew his intentions were not to benefit the welfare of our children, but a way of having continuous control over me. The relationship with Mr. Blue would prove to be just what I needed: a man who was not afraid of Mr. Cain and one who would tell me what to do to stop a stalker, Mr. Nonchalant, from continuing to contact me.

During a breakup with Mr. Cain, I was asked to join my cousin on a double date with Mr. Nonchalant who was also on a break from his girlfriend. We got along well and dated briefly, but ultimately, we both returned to our respective relationships. Years later, while separated from Mr. Cain, because of his many indiscretions, I revisited the relationship with Mr. Nonchalant, just to see where our relationship would go. I believe that sometimes if things start and don't finish in a relationship, you may revisit the relationship later during your journey of life.

Mr. Nonchalant was funny, a little cocky, and was not afraid to speak up or defend me. One day after my divorce from Mr. Cain was finalized, he stopped by unannounced at my momma's house. He was not acting like the same guy that I knew. His tone of speech was lower and monotonous, and he was stuttering as he spoke. I tried to get him to leave, but he wouldn't. My brother, who was outside with his friends, knew Mr. Nonchalant and felt comfortable with me being alone with him, but little did he know I needed to be rescued again. My daughters were playing a game and Mr. Nonchalant joined them. When it was bedtime for the girls, they went to bed while I tried to be crafty about getting him out of my house. He kept babbling and when my brother walked through the door to check on us, I tried to give him an eye signal that I was not comfortable. I must have been too subtle because my brother did not notice my silent cry for help.

After my brother left to go back outside with his friends, Mr. Nonchalant forcefully pulled me by my arm into the den area and, ignoring my pleas, violently pressed me against the sofa, pulled my panties down, and forced himself on me. I desperately tried to stop him but he overpowered me; I did not stand a chance. It shocked me that he would violate both my trust and my body and appeared to have no empathy as he fulfilled his malicious desires. He got up as if he had done nothing wrong and went back to talking to me like we were friends. Once again, I was overpowered by a man. After this traumatic event, I went on with my life as if nothing ever happened. I did not want to be treated as if I could have been responsible for the rape that was an obvious violation of my temple. I wondered if he somehow felt justified in his actions and did not consider this encounter to be a rape and even thought I didn't blame myself or anyone else for what happened to me, but I wished my brother would have sensed my uneasiness with Mr. Nonchalant.

I never once considered telling anyone about the rape because I was ashamed and did not want to recall anything about the incident. I thought he was a nice guy, so why would he do that to me?! If I had to replay this situation again, I would have yelled out as loudly as possible to draw attention at any cost. This experience left me feeling numb, but not numb enough to stop myself from

WHEN THE CURTAIN FALLS

moving forward with another relationship and searching for love once again.

Growth 101- It is important to admit the trauma you have experienced. Recovery becomes more challenging when you deny the inherent trauma caused by a violation.

At this point of my journey, Mr. Blue was officially on the scene. I only revealed to him that a man from my past kept calling me after I asked him not to call anymore. He told me to change my number, and I did. Mr. Blue was looking rather favorable as a prospective love interest, and he appeared to be willing to offer support and protect me and my girls. We experienced many highs and lows throughout our relationship. Red flags were present from the beginning, but because I felt the need to have a man in my life as a protector, I simply ignored them all.

Early in our relationship, I went to a seafood restaurant and came back with dinner for the evening. Over the course of the night he became angry and opinionated about how I disciplined one of my daughters and took it upon himself to interject his thoughts. This was my first glimpse of a curtain that would need to fall. He did not like that I dared to disagree with him as he told me how to "properly" discipline my daughters. This was a touchy subject for me because I was not ready for any other man, other than their father, to take on the disciplinarian role in their lives and I felt emboldened to stand up for my convictions. After I expressed my concerns to him, I tried to hand him his dinner. He threw the shrimp meal on my front porch and left. I thought he was crazy! I should have run then, but I decided to give him another chance. He reminded me of a snake slithering his way back into my life repeatedly.

When I finally decided to break up with him, he came to my job, pulled his police car onto the curb and when he approached my Assistant Principal, he asked, "Where is that mean lady, Ms. Thomas?" Unfortunately, I had a tendency of finding stalkers and men who did not want to let me go. I was also very fearful and not healed from the pain that I had previously endured as a victim of domestic violence. Throughout the duration of the nineteen years that we were together, I regrettably kept him around, in part, to assist me financially. He pitched in to help me and my daughters, but was not providing for all our financial needs. One example of his financial support was when he purchased a washer and dryer for us after he had taken a new assignment overseas. He contributed Christmas gifts each year to my daughters, had talks with them and tried to help when I needed support while he was in town. He traveled back and forth for work, but he flew me to Budapest, Vienna, and Paris! These were the first opportunities I had to fly on an airplane, let alone travel abroad. I was so excited about each of our trips.

My first flight was an international vacation to Paris. During the Paris getaway, I noticed he was on his phone quite a few times. I have an Inspector Gadget nature which allows me to pick up on certain things. The realization that he was distracted by his phone may have also been God's power of discernment alerting me to the truth about his life. Curious about what could be more enthralling than our lover's trip to Paris, I innocently asked him who was he talking to. He responded by becoming extremely irritated with me and became aggressive with his words and his behavior. His aggressive words and behavior heightened his replies.

Part of me questioned his ability to afford the trip in the first place, because I knew it was awfully expensive to take a European vacation. I did not voice this concern to him because of the way he was acting toward me as we walked back to the hotel. He seemed annoyed and I suspected he was tired from our trip into the city. As we walked through the entrance of our hotel, he was cursing at me and exhibiting very aggressive behavior. As we headed to our room and as the elevator doors closed, he was irrationally furious, which I've come to recognize as the typical behavior of a pathological liar. By the time we made it into our hotel room, I was exhausted. The weather was rainy and miserable and I was disappointed at the underwhelming start to our vacation, I just wanted to take a shower and try to forget Mr. Blue's alarmingly hostile behavior from earlier that day.

I entered the bathroom and quietly breathed a sigh of relief as I prepared to wash away the strife of the day with a relaxing shower. Suddenly, the man I thought I knew appeared out of thin air, as jarring and abrasive as a bolt of lightning. He barged into the bathroom and swiftly ripped opened the shower curtain. I was in total shock. Frozen in fear while trapped within the miniscule confines of the Parisian shower, I screamed as he began to viciously beat me. Unrelenting in his anger, he savagely abused me as I cried out for mercy. The rooms in our hotel were tiny, so neighboring guests on our floor could undoubtedly hear what was happening within our suite. While his tall, slender, brawny frame loomed over my helpless body, he barked, "Shut your mouth before someone comes in here thinking I am killing you!" In that moment, I wept and feared for my life.

There I was again in 2001 experiencing domestic violence at the hands of a man. He acted as if he were insane. He snapped and turned into a monster; a disturbed man who I hardly recognized. In my mind, I was trying to find excuses for his behavior towards me. The problem that I had was that I always wanted to find the good in people — not the bad. I could clearly see there was an extra element of stress behind his actions, but I still felt he was a little too unstable. I found myself in total disbelief about what I experienced in that hotel bathroom. I was helpless in a foreign country, with nowhere to run and no one to turn to. After his violent outburst, we did not speak to one another for a while. Still, I was trying to be optimistic about my first trip to Paris. I naturally assumed there were things we would do together while in this amazing city. Unfortunately, because of limited funds, I walked the streets of Paris in disappointment.

This beautiful city that some refer to as the "City of Lights" became a disillusioned city of darkness for me. I will never forget the pain of this experience. The Eiffel Tower, Versailles Palace, Luxembourg Gardens, and Arc de Triomphe were incredible places I would only get a glimpse of by seeing them on gift shop postcards or by listlessly walking near them as I wandered through the city. The Musee d'Orsay houses amazing artwork beneath a glass ceiling with creations from Monet, Van Gogh, Seurat, Renoir, and many other famous artists. It would have been a dream come true to visit the gallery, yet here I was — so close, yet so far away.

Mr. Blue was a police officer when I met him and I have a lot of respect for the men and women in uniform, but I was now seeing the opposite spectrum of the blue and white. I was a domestic violence survivor who left a volatile and tumultuous relationship and unwittingly ended up with someone who was abusing me again. Traumatized by the entire ordeal, I attempted to sleep on the floor the night before we left Paris. Mr. Blue forced me to sleep in the same bed with him, but I did not want to be near this monster. When this fateful trip was mercifully over, I was so happy to get back on United States soil. I promised myself that I would never go out of the country with him again. My momma and daughters were picking us up from the airport. Of course, I did not want anyone to know about the abuse that transpired, so I had to act like my trip to Paris was the vacation of a lifetime. Many consider Paris to be the "City of Romance", but for me it turned out to be the "City of Terror".

There was a lot of mystery surrounding Mr. Blue. I only met one of his brothers during the entire time we dated. I spoke to his mother and sons on the phone twice, but I never visited his physical address. These red flags combined with the domestic abuse, should have been my signs to run, but I stayed. He always had good reasons for me to stick around, and it was the first time I was in a relationship with a man who could help me financially. The child support I was receiving from Mr. Cain was very inconsistent, and by the time I received funds from him I would have already needed to borrow multiple loans from several companies to provide for my family. Most times, I had to pay back the various loan companies with finances received from child support. Despite my vow to never leave the country with this man again, I packed for another trip with Mr. Blue to Budapest, Hungary. At this stage in my life, money, and cars impressed me. I would have sacrificed my soul to be with a man who was providing me with great sex and a touch of the finer things in life.

During our trip to Budapest, I mastered the art of dealing with Mr. Blue. I learned his triggers and had them down to a science. I would be extremely quiet to avoid any conflicts. Our journey to Budapest would prove to be better than the hellish ordeal sustained in Paris, but I witnessed signs of his instability. He became moody and did not speak to me after going out on the town, but at least he did not hit me. Our third and final trip together was to Vienna in Austria. When I arrived, there was a beautiful brown fur salon mink fur A-line coat waiting on the bed for me. It was near Thanksgiving, and my birthday was on November 24th. My co-workers at the time thought that there would be a proposal on this trip, but thank God there was not. This was the first time I was not with my family on my birthday or such a meaningful holiday as Thanksgiving. My family was extremely protective of me because of my naïve nature. I always asked Momma and my daughters before going if they were okay with me leaving, and of course they wanted me to be happy. They believed I was happy with him, so they would agree.

Early one morning on a snowy day, we ventured into the town of Vienna for a scenic walk. On our way back to the hotel he started an argument. He got angry and walked ahead of me, way ahead of me, as heavy snow fell from the sky. I could not even see in front of me as I walked. I was so scared. He deliberately abandoned me in a foreign country while I was away from my family, and so close to the holidays and my birthday. Distraught, I prayed, "God, if you get me home safely I will never go on another trip with this man again." We did not go on another vacation together. Throughout our relationship, I always knew there was another side to Mr. Blue. He would come and go as he pleased, staying with me a few nights, and then leaving for a few nights with good explanations.

His line of work created a simple way to conceal his double life. As time passed, I stumbled upon evidence that he was living with another woman. Retrospectively, I believe I was being led by a higher power to the exact location where he lived with this other woman and his children. I remember riding with him one day through a small run down town and two years later discovered that this was the town where he lived. One thing that troubles me the most is a liar. I have a low tolerance for liars. One night he lied to me, and I called him out on it. I wanted the truth. He revealed he was living in an old trailer and recently bought a new one, but he told me he was not living with another woman. The only proof I had of his infidelity was the fact that I caught him there. A good liar or schemer can always get out of a lie and that time, he did just that. I did some research which ultimately led me to the location of the other woman. I found out that he had two daughters, when he told me he only had one.

After finding this information and while he was on a tour out of the country, I drove to the house of his other woman, and I nervously knocked on the door. She was extremely nice and just seemed broken down. She asked me if I was his wife and then told me she thought he loved me — not her. I felt awful. She also revealed to me the horrific abuse that she had endured at his hands. Although she suffered abuse, she was still in love with him. I was surprised to find myself playing a role in this warped "love triangle". Finding myself in a relationship filled with deception and lies, I convinced myself to stay with him because I did not want to look like a fool to the public. I felt I had to uphold a certain image. I was a little afraid of Mr. Blue, but after speaking to his other woman, I knew I was ready to end our relationship. I should have left him for many reasons prior to this, but there was one story that I did not want anyone to ever find out about. I was hiding behind a curtain of secrets.

Early one Sunday morning, I remember my daughter coming to me and saying, "Momma, Mr. Blue touched me". I froze. Deeply concerned, I said to her, "What did you say? Excuse me, what did you just say? What happened?" This was crazy. This was a man that I trusted to be around my children. He was their father figure. The truth of the matter was that he was a monster that would leave my loving relationship with my daughters bankrupt for many years to come because of poor judgement on my part. I was thinking only of my sexual desires and needs, and placing them before my children.

After this revelation from my daughter, I remember Mr. Blue talking to Mr. Cain in the front of the house. Mr. Blue would not tell me what they discussed. To this day, I wonder if their conversation went like this: "You better not put your hands on my daughters. If you do, I *will* kill you." I was trying to listen to them from the window, but I could not hear the actual conversation. I could only decipher the sounds of raised voices. Mr. Blue came back into the house and seemed a little startled that someone was on to him, but I wasn't. My Achilles heel was trusting people too much. As a mother, I made the biggest mistake of my life. I put this perpetrator in the presence of my young daughters and even asked them, "Are you comfortable with Mr. Blue in our home?" Lord, what the hell was I thinking? I removed him from my home, but eventually allowed him to come back.

Of course, he never violated my daughters again, but they told me he would harass them. After they revealed this to me, I did not want anyone to ever think or know that "Ms. Perfect" had any part in these misdeeds. Allow me to break it down for you: I was being selfish and thinking about the superficial desires of my flesh. I must have lost my mind! Even my daughters felt like I chose a man over them. I looked back on the events that occurred and said, "Lord, I needed an intervention." I did not know where to turn. My momma has always offered me guidance, so of course I made her aware of the situation. I felt as if I was getting conflicting information, so I was confused and totally in disbelief that this could happen to my family. This curtain eventually fell, and I am telling my story to help share the pain that it causes a family when we hide behind the curtain of our imperfections.

Growth 101 – A perpetrator is charismatic and an everyday person who earns the trust of others. They could be the staff at your child's school, they could be the coach, the music teacher, or a police officer. They could be the person at your church, they could be the babysitter, or they could be your own family member. Never hide the offense because this is how children become damaged adults.

We are now just dealing with a lot of the trauma caused during my daughters' childhood. Because I was hiding behind the curtain, my daughters did not receive counseling for the violations that occurred, and Mr. Blue should have never been allowed back into my home.

My daughters went from elementary school through high school consistently making honor roll, being involved in organizations, and taking part in sports — all the while having been molested. Through all the trauma that I, as a mother, did not protect them from, they persevered and made me proud. My children proved to be more resilient than I was. I was stressed out from raising three daughters as a single mother, but I never gave up. I fought hard for our lives, no matter what pressures I faced financially. It was exceedingly difficult to put three girls through private school and simultaneously be a paraprofessional. I received support through the Catholic Diocese of Savannah, which helped with various aspects of tuition and books. Still, it was my responsibility to come up with the remaining balance for tuition and book fees. As mentioned previously, their child support payments were not coming regularly and my salary at the time was roughly $10.50 an hour.

When I look back on these struggles, I often wondered how we survived, but now I know it was by God's grace and mercy. My daughters have expressed to me that, while they were growing up, I would sometimes be verbally abusive towards them. I repeated the cycle of childhood and marital abuse. I didn't receive appropriate counseling so I was afraid for me and for my daughters.

Growth 101- Parenting classes would have been a great resource, in addition to individual counseling, therapy, spiritual counseling, Christian life coaching, and budgeting classes.

Growth 101- You may not know what another person is capable of, but any signs that alert you to the possibility that you've brought an unstable person into your life should resonate with you. Once you discern that danger, get out of it and save your family from any harm that could negatively affect the next generation.

Because of his training as a police officer, Mr. Blue was extremely calculating, conniving, and skilled at deception and I was oblivious to his predatory behavior. When discussing their past traumas with me as adults, my girls made me aware of all sorts of activity that I was not aware of while it was occurring. For example, they told me that while I was in my night classes, Mr. Blue would use that time as his opportunity for evil. He would say, "Your mom won't be mad...", and then fondle them. They told me that he often looked at them inappropriately and would glare at them as if to say, "I cannot wait to be alone with you," but I never picked up on his misplaced gazes.

One of my daughters recalled a time when she was in the 10th grade and he was bothering her by kissing her on the neck and touching her legs. She always wanted to be away from the house, and she later told me he was the reason. My daughter locked her bedroom door at night because she was so afraid of him. They collectively described a time when they asked me if they could go to the movies on their own. I told them, "Sure. Mr. Blue will be there off duty." My daughter turned to me and said, "Momma...", and then looked at her sisters with an expression that read, "Really? We will be better because he is there?" I had no idea how un-reassuring that sounded to my innocent daughters who he was molesting.

I can now see how I was manipulated. He portrayed himself as a father figure to get my daughters alone with him under the pretense that he was helping me with discipline and looking out for our best interests. I was overwhelmed with life and eager to accept aid from someone I trusted. My children loved this man! We had been together as a couple for so many years as they were growing up and they trusted us to look out for them. Mr. Blue's behavior made it difficult for them to keep their faith in us. One of my girls switched moods and would become inexplicably defensive. She wouldn't allow anyone to hug her or be near her, but I thought it was just one of her personality traits. In reality, this was a defense mechanism that she developed and held onto for much of her life, just like my momma.

I praise God that my daughters could forgive me for the years of their childhood that were torturous because of, in part, my poor judgment as their mother and protector. I was not thinking about my children's welfare. I chose a man over my family, and there came a time when I had to come clean and take responsibility for that. When my daughters were adults, I asked them, "Why didn't you guys tell me about this when it first began? Why did you wait so many years to reveal what you were dealing with regularly?" I tried so hard to do right by my girls and protect them. I simply could not fathom how this atrocity could happen without my Inspector Gadget instincts picking up on the danger.

When they were emotionally ready to delve into this period of their lives, my daughters revealed truths that were suppressed for over twenty-five years. Mr. Blue was an opportunistic predator who sensed my vulnerabilities and took full advantage of my family. Whenever anyone wanted to visit me or tried to get close to my daughters, he would speak ill against them. Through my experiences, I learned that perpetrators try to isolate you and your children. He was craftily grooming my daughters. Due to his mental manipulation, I was in denial about the abuse my children endured. The very thought made me numb.

I had people in my life who tried to warn me about him, but their concerns fell on deaf ears. My brother and his wife never liked him. They were suspicious of him and constantly asked the children if anyone had been bothering them or touching them inappropriately. My girls would protect me by saying no. I had no idea these conversations between them were going on. As if grappling with these truths weren't enough, I received yet another bombshell.

While one of my girls was visiting me about three decades after this time, we had a conversation about the abuse. She mustered up the courage to say, "Momma...somebody else molested me." This admission floored me. I knew my daughter would not open up right away, so I told her, "Sweetheart, when you are ready, we can talk about it." I did not want to pressure her into discussing any details that she was not prepared to bring back up; I simply consoled her. Still, I was baffled by this bombshell and tried to figure out who could have done this to her.

About a week later, a family member's name dropped in my spirit and a few days after that, God revealed to me exactly who it was. I called my daughter and asked her if the perpetrator was Mr. Sly. Weeping, she said, "Momma... yes. How did you know?" I started screaming, crying, and thanking God for revealing that person to me. I was in pain for my daughter because now I finally understood why she was the way she was.

With hindsight as a vantage point, I believe with all my heart and soul that I would have killed Mr. Blue had I known the truth about what was happening. My children would be without their mother and the man who played the role of their father for so many years. I believe I found out years after the abuse occurred so that I would not cause deeper psychological damage than what they had already endured. I have subsequently forgiven all the men who have hurt me and my family during my lifetime. I have learned valuable lessons from my experiences, and I am profoundly grateful for every bit of wisdom that I gained.

Growth 101 - It is important to develop a non-threatening relationship with your children; one that fosters an environment where they feel comfortable talking with you about anything. More importantly, it is imperative that as parents we listen and create an environment in which the parent and child experience ritual activities together because this allows them to be in the moment together forming a unique and long-lasting bond. Children love spending quality time with their parents. It provides them the opportunity to bloom and feel loved. The connection starts with listening and acknowledging your child's feelings. Show them that you are there to assist with their needs.

One daughter said to me, "Momma, as African-Americans we were raised to believe that children should stay in "a child's place" and not speak unless spoken to. We were taught not to express our feelings. You told us to just hold in our emotions until years later when the pots have simmered and then boiled over." She further explained that parents should speak to their children everyday about their feelings and have conversations about what is happening in their lives. This communication would foster the security needed for children to come to their parents about anything. I lacked this understanding as a young parent and handled the situation the way my momma would have in the same circumstance. I was so busy trying to provide for them and have a life that I missed important signs that were right before my eyes.

I was a strong disciplinarian; my children couldn't even spend the night with their friends. I tried to watch them very closely, yet they were taken advantage of inside of a place where they should have felt safe and protected -- home. I allowed Mr. Blue back into our lives and, looking back, I can see the negative impact that my actions had on my daughters. They were bitter and hated me because I chose my drug at the time (which was a man) over them. I provided my children with shelter, food, and clothing, but their environment proved to be toxic.

WHEN THE CURTAIN FALLS

After finding out about the molestations, I should have pressed charges against Mr. Blue. He was a man in uniform who worked on a day-to-day basis in the public eye who took an oath to protect and serve. I took responsibility for the pain I caused my daughters by allowing this man to enter our home. I admitted, to myself and to my children, that I had made a poor decision and apologized for the pain and suffering I caused in their lives. I regretted dropping the ball in keeping my children safe and I had to take a closer look at the generational patterns that plagued my family.

In order for me to end this pattern, I had to ask myself some tough questions. How did this happen without me noticing the signs? Why did I allow him to come back into our lives after my daughters told me what happened? What could I do to make this situation better? What have I learned from this as a mother? I also wrote a list of reasons I had to assume accountability for this situation. We could not afford for this generational pattern to go any further. It needed to end right here.

Over time, my daughters and I have spoken at length about their experiences. We have had conversations both together and separately and are currently in counseling to help us build a stronger bond. This trauma put a significant strain on our relationship when my daughters were in high school. It was a crucial time when they needed me the most. Sometimes, I checked out on them because I was still in a relationship with the monster. Little did I know God was building my strength and character so that I could finally be who I was ordained to be.

A Shimmer of Light

⚜

My story began in the Georgia Infirmary Hospital in
Savannah, Georgia. This was the first hospital in the
United States for African Americans. I was born on
November 24, 1964, to a twenty-one-year-old African American
mother and a twenty-three-year-old African American father. My
momma was reared by her aunt. As she grew older, she lived with
a constant fear of being molested by her aunt's husband. This negatively affected her life, and ultimately mine as well. We were both
characters in the same script, just in different acts. I was born in the
same year that the landmark Civil Rights and Labor Laws were en-
acted, which outlawed discrimination based on race, color, religion, sex, and national origin. Later, sexual orientation and gender
identity protections were signed into law.

As a child, I remember riding in the car with my aunt and uncle on a bright Sunday afternoon. My uncle pulled into a white-
owned gas station and the attendant who was pumping our gas
could not stop looking at me because of my light complexion. He

clearly thought that I was Caucasian with a Black family. He allowed my uncle to drive away without paying for the gas! This remained a running joke for decades within our family. Momma told me that there were rumors swirling around the city from family members and friends. They said that because my complexion was light that I was the "milk man's baby" or the "postman's baby". These terms were used to imply that a woman had an affair outside of her marriage and did not know the identity of her child's father, or that a child was of mixed race because of the color of an African American child's skin.

I knew early on that I looked different from the rest of my family. I received my complexion from my momma's grandfather, who was white, and from my grandfather's father who was Irish and his mother who was a Cherokee Indian. The color gene skipped generations, as it often does and in some ways having a light complexion was such a bumpy and tough road for me. I felt as if I did not totally fit in because of my skin color and many people that I've encountered did not know how to categorize me upon first meeting me.

I remember going to my aunt's house and my cousin said to me, "Come here, white girl!" The cousins who were my age would often introduce me as their "white cousin" and when my brother introduced me to people, they would say, "That is NOT your sister, Robert!" Some would go as far to say, "She's too pretty to be YOUR sister." I hated when people said that because I know it made my brother feel bad. When I met new friends, the first questions they would ask me were, "Are you mixed? Is that your real hair?" Keep in mind, I was born in the early sixties. I always felt different and was often treated as an outcast.

My father met my momma at a basketball game at S. C. Johnson High School. He caught a glimpse of her and then she faded into the crowd. Transfixed by her beauty, he ventured out into the crowd to find her and ask her for her name. They dated two years before getting married. Momma was eighteen years old, and her aunt had to sign for her to get married. After their wedding, they lived with my momma's brother and his wife. My dad had not finished high school because other students picked on him because of the shoes he wore.

As a young man, he found work so that he could split bills with my aunt and uncle. Momma became pregnant soon after, but unfortunately her first-born baby died in utero. She had to carry the deceased baby full term. She took the death of her first child extremely hard but became pregnant with her second child soon after. That child would be another son, and then nineteen months later I arrived.

Momma was a homemaker, and my daddy worked on the railroad until he decided to follow his heart into the fishing and shrimping industry. Momma enjoyed school and was an excellent student who wanted to become a nurse. She deferred her dream in order to assist my father with building the family business and received her CNA license later in life to support herself and my younger brother. Growing up, I had an extraordinarily strong family unit and never witnessed my parents arguing or fighting. I got married at nineteen years of age, and like my parents, married my high school sweetheart.

As a little girl, I was shy and quiet and my feelings were easily hurt. I was soft-spoken and compassionate. I attended Catholic School from kindergarten through 12th grade. Catholicism was deeply embedded into the very fiber of my being, and I was one of the few African American students in my classes throughout my school years. I attended an African American church, so I was exposed to both white and black cultures.

One day before dismissal as a kindergarten student, Momma arrived to pick me up and one of my classmates asked if she was my nanny. I was terribly upset that she thought my momma was my maid. I became sensitive to racism and had a keen awareness of it within social contexts. Dr. Martin Luther King Jr. was my hero. As a prominent advocate for civil rights within the public eye, I looked up to him and eventually adopted his non-violent teachings.

Throughout my life, I have been told by many men that I am easy to love. I believe this to be true, but a lot of my boyfriends fought the feeling of loving me. Perhaps they thought they were not worthy to have me. They could not believe I was a normal woman despite the physical beauty God had given me. I often received comments like, "You're nothing like I thought you would be! Most red women are stuck up." I did not believe it when they complimented me. My mother always told me, "Do not let your color go to your head. You are no better than my other children." She kept me grounded. I just wanted to give love and be loved in return.

I really enjoyed making friends as a little girl. I remember when I allowed a so-called friend into my bedroom and she saw a necklace that she liked. It was a beautiful green sapphire necklace given to me by my aunt and it was near and dear to my heart. When I walked out of my room, she coveted my necklace and decided she wanted it for herself. After my "friend" left, I noticed it was missing. I contacted her to return it, and her sister told me she would get it back for me and she did. This was not an isolated incident and would be repeated during my sophomore year of high school.

My brother was dating a genuinely nice young woman who attended the same high school as me. We were good friends and her mom was crazy about my brother. We also had a great relationship with her mother. This girl was my best friend for two years and she even introduced me to my boyfriend during high school, who later became my husband. We were walking down Broughton Street with several girls during our free time, and my future husband was downtown at the same time. He said, "Who is she? The one with the two ponytails--I like her." Then my best friend took it upon herself to set up our first meeting. When I found out what she was planning, I told her I did not know him. Our friends told me, "That is Mr. Cain! He dresses so well and ALL the girls want him! Girl, he SO FINE! You better talk to him!" Their words rang in my ears for many years to come.

After my best friend introduced me to him. . . well, the rest is history. My best friend continued to date my brother and we would often go places together. We incorporated her into our family functions and vice versa. What I didn't know was that she was secretly meeting with my boyfriend behind my back. The same boyfriend that she introduced me to, she obviously had a crush on. My brother told me about an incident that should have alerted us to their indiscretions.

One evening after school he went to her house to spend time with her and found my boyfriend there when he arrived. We brushed it off, but I think he knew there was more going on between them. My brother never cared for my boyfriend, and neither did any of my friends. That was a huge red flag that I ignored.

Growth 101 - Listen to friends and family who love you and who are looking objectively from a fresh pair of lenses. They may truly have insight into your situation but prefer not to reveal information or advice. If given the chance to express their opinions, their advice could save you from heartache or even save your life. Your family often sees things you may not be aware of.

My sophomore year of high school would prove to be the start of many poor choices to come. I was in love, and that was where my focus went. I listened to love songs constantly and simply loved being "in love". Some of these experiences were part of my path in life, but some of the pit falls could have been avoided. I came home from school one day and my dad had just purchased a new car for me. This generous gift became a huge mistake because I used it to travel to West Savannah when I was supposed to be other places. My friends and I would go all over town during our open-campus privilege breaks and come back to class a little late.

Despite exploring my newfound freedom, my grades were good. On one of my outings, my boyfriend and I decided to go to the state fair. My best friend told me she wanted to go with us, and I obliged. We went to the fairgrounds together but, due to my fear of heights, I did not enjoy going on rides that were high off the ground. My friend did not share the same phobia, so she and Mr. Cain went on rides together and had a great time. I did not say anything to them about how uncomfortable they made me feel and after we left the fair, we dropped her off at her house. As she exited the car, she kissed him on his lips. I thought to myself, "What is she doing?!" She knew exactly what she was doing.

As time went on, my boyfriend and I continued to date one another and I continued to love my best friend. I would take her places with my family and she did the same for me. Little did I know, my life was about to be forever changed. My boyfriend's cousin had an apartment and we went there to hang out one afternoon. The two of us were lying in the bedroom talking and I happened to be telling him a story that involved my best friend. He became frustrated and said to me, "I am tired of you talking about her. She *is not* your best friend." I was caught off guard. Innocently I asked, "Why would you say that? Do you just not like her?" He hesitated for a moment and then admitted something that was devastating to me as a young woman trying to find her way in this world. He told me he was having sex with her. I was furious. By this time, I had already lost my virginity to him. He was a senior in high school, and I was just a sophomore.

When we first started dating, I fell in love with him instantly. I had my first sexual experience with him, which was not pleasant. Still, I was shocked by this news and I was not prepared to deal with it. I confronted her, but one major problem was that I did not handle my boyfriend the way I should have after finding out about their affair. I should have booted him too instead of just my friend. This revelation was devastating to our group of friends. I was betrayed by two people who I thought I could rely on. This experience heightened my distrust of other women. To make matters worse, it turned out that my boyfriend's on-again, off-again ex-girlfriend was pregnant! He did not think the child was his, but the baby was his and looked exactly like him. His child became incredibly special to me.

After learning about his extracurricular activities, one of my friends who was already sexually active took me to get birth control pills. Momma found out and was upset that I made this decision without her consent. At the time, anyone could go to the clinic and receive contraceptives. I was extremely naïve and we did not discuss sex in my home. I was raised to be a nice little Catholic girl. The curtains in my life were deteriorating, and I tried to protect myself from being exposed as "less than pure", especially considering Mr. Cain's infidelity. Momma was adamant that she did not want me to date Mr. Cain, in part because he was a few years older than me.

Defiant and in love, I told her that if she stopped me from seeing him I was going to sneak around and be with him anyway.

My brother did not like my boyfriend because he could tell that Mr. Cain was a Casanova-type who just loved the women. That was not what I wanted. I did not see that type of character within my family. My dad was committed to my momma and treated her like a queen (or so it appeared). Despite my attempt to use wisdom as a teen, by my senior year of high school I became a statistic. I became pregnant but had an abortion. I repented and asked God for forgiveness. Momma did not allow me to be a debutante because of my irresponsible behavior. I was still given the opportunity to go off to college, but I was neither mature nor focused enough for this endeavor because I wanted to be at home in Savannah with my first love.

Mr. Cain wanted me to go to school and get my degree and told me we would get married once I finished college. I had average intelligence as a student, but I wanted to be super smart. I realized that with God all things are possible. I had problems comprehending the curriculum during my elementary years because I simply did not enjoy reading. Momma had me academically tested and when the scores came back, my teacher told my momma that there was nothing wrong with me except a noticeable lack of self-confidence. I was never the smartest girl in the classroom, but I knew I was capable. Unfortunately, I was a poor test taker.

In my school, they grouped us according to our standardized test scores. My scores were low and placed me in the lowest group

— the D group. This academic separation caused me to develop limited English skills. I took a few writing classes in high school, but I missed out on some of the advanced courses that the other young women were offered because of the way the school grouped us. This proved to be detrimental during my college years. I ventured into higher education ill-prepared to write college-level papers and possessed a weak literary background. When I enrolled in my university, I was placed in a developmental studies course and failed the writing test. I didn't know how to express myself well in written form and I did not understand the concept of writing a five-paragraph essay. When I took my developmental studies course, I selected a teacher who was the "easiest English instructor." I avoided the tougher professors and this decision served me poorly because I did not gain the skills required to pass my tests. I ruined my opportunity to attend that university and had to come home after only one year of college.

Growth 101 - My advice to undergraduate students is to take courses taught by disciplined instructors who demand excellence from their students.

After returning home to Savannah, I remember going to the University of Georgia to visit a friend of mine. I spotted a professor whose class I avoided taking and I was embarrassed when she recognized me. She told me, "You should have taken my class. If you had, I think you would have passed your writing test." I felt humiliation spread through my body and that encounter haunted me for years. I was forced to drop out of college because I was not focused on my studies and only wanted to focus on my relationship with Mr. Cain. I desperately wanted to be his wife and start our own family. Growing up, I watched how my momma cared for my father and her children and I wanted to be just like her.

Despite my interest in domestic life, I always believed that there was an intelligent, self-confident, and independent leader within and I had a burning desire to do something impactful in my life. After all, I looked up to Dr. Martin Luther King Jr. and hoped to emulate him in some ways. I discovered an innate passion for training and mentoring those who I could positively influence when I went above and beyond to assist new employees at work. My peers and supervisors wanted to mentor me and push me to a higher level. Dr. Prince Jackson and Gwendolyn Goodman were consistent in offering guidance and pouring into my spirit. Even with their loving mentorship, I still did not trust my own abilities. I lacked self-confidence, and the sting of domestic violence left me emotionally bankrupt. It was almost as if I had forgotten how to dream, but God allowed me to peep through the curtain that obstructed my view and I saw education through the open window. As we grow, our talents grow, and as we blossom, our gifts and talents develop. I became passionate about helping children flourish and knew teaching was my God given talent. We always had children in my home because in my mind, it was safer to host my children's friends at our house rather than let them play in the homes of people I did not know well. This allowed me to keep a watchful eye on my girls.

Determined to fulfill my purpose, I followed my spirit and enrolled in college for the second time. I became pregnant and unable to complete the semester due to being hospitalized. Naïve to the policy and just lacking wisdom and sound guidance, I did not withdraw properly which left me with low grades on my transcript. I was able to get what was called a fresh start from Armstrong State Atlantic University many years later affording me a third chance which would prove to be the charm. I finally learned how to compose college-level papers once I entered Savannah State University, but I still needed to learn many valuable fundamentals that would better prepare me for the future that lied ahead.

During my senior year of college, administrators who worked in the registrar's office realized I never took the Regents exam which was an exam used to measure student achievement in college-level courses. I was already in my senior year and was ordered by the registrar's office to take this exam during the middle of the testing session. Whenever I took a standardized test, I became anxious and was distracted by the slightest noise. After many years of formal education, I grew to recognize this trait as test anxiety. Because I was unprepared for this change of events, I ran out of time and failed the test.

Once again, I had to register for a preparatory course that would serve a purpose later in my life. My professor told me, "Redina, you will not pass all parts of the test. No one has ever completed all three sections and passed after failing." Many students knew what these rudimentary classes were and they often stared or laughed at the students who took them. Well, one thing I never lacked was determination. I buckled down, applied myself to my studies, passed all three sections of the Regents exam and graduated on time, which was a major accomplishment for me! Overcoming my test anxiety was difficult, but I was spurred on by my previous shortcomings in this area.

When I took the teacher exam to teach high school English, I failed the examination by one point in critical thinking. It took me three attempts to earn my leadership certificate, but I refused to give up. When I took my teacher exams, whenever it was possible, I sat in the back. My life had been impacted by a few brilliant administrators whom I loved dearly. The late Gwendolyn Goodman was someone I truly admired. She encouraged me to keep pushing and inspired me to go back to school to get my teaching degree. She always told me how proud she was of my ability to raise my daughters after having dealt with the abuse I encountered. Another one of my mentors, Dr. Toney Jordan, gave me my first contracted teaching position. He also spoke life into me and helped reform my damaged perspective on men created by the ones who caused me harm. I remember him telling me, "Mrs. Thomas, this man did something good for you, he gave you three beautiful daughters." This simple statement made me remember how blessed I was to have my precious family.

As a young woman, my momma dreamed of forming a better relationship with her father. She knew him, but he lived in another state. When my grandfather wanted to move back to Savannah,

Momma made it possible by allowing him to move in with us. She also allowed her siblings to visit us and supported them during their transitions to Savannah. On the surface, my uncle seemed to be a genuinely nice and caring man. He always showed love and affection to us and he got along extremely well with my father. For a while, we were a happy family. My dad had help on his shrimp boats, and my momma was able to spend quality time with her father and siblings. My momma adored her family and I learned to appreciate, love, and assist the ones I cared about by watching her give her heart and soul to us. Her inspiring example created a set of standards that I desired to uphold. My blissful vision of family life would one day clash with the traumatic environment that would be unleashed during my marriage. Unfortunately, what we did not know was that one of Momma's siblings would be a part of a nightmare. My beloved uncle was a troubled man who kept his dark secrets hidden from us.

When I first began dating Mr. Cain, my uncle took me to the park to talk to me and give me some advice on how to carry myself as a young woman in love. He also took it upon himself to become friends with my boyfriend. After gaining our trust, he surprised me by telling my dad that Mr. Cain smoked marijuana. My father was upset by this information and I didn't understand why my uncle would do this when he knew it would cause problems for me. He was both looking out for me and planting seeds of discord that would bloom and work in his favor.

One evening, my brother and I were lying next to each other on my brother's bed while my uncle watched TV in the bedroom with us. My uncle told me, "I want you to sleep in the bed with me. If you don't, I am going to sleep in your room with you." As a young girl, I knew he was not allowed into my bedroom. Instead, we slept in my brother's bed. He grabbed my hand and forced me to play with his penis. When my dad woke up the next morning and found me in bed with my uncle, I remember my dad yelling, screaming, and cursing at him. "What are you doing in bed with my daughter?" My father was seething with rage when he told my uncle that he could no longer stay with us. "Sleep on the boat!" he yelled.

Years after that incident, my brother had a health crisis and, he was distraught and kept confessing all the horrible things my uncle had done to both of us. I wondered if my uncle preyed on anyone else while he was living alone on that shrimp boat. He had a darkness about him that hurt many women in his lifetime and even though I never confronted him about the things he had done, I genuinely wished for that opportunity. I kept these secrets to myself, but I didn't trust him around my cousins who still viewed him as their loving uncle. There are generational patterns that can spread within our families and even if we have no idea how or when these patterns may have first taken root, they have the propensity to corrupt future generations if left hidden behind a curtain.

Growth 101 - One must be aware of generational patterns and be willing to have brave conversations with those who understand the damage they cause when passed through generations. We must learn how to deal with emotions using healthy coping mechanisms which can be demonstrated by positive role models. It helps to listen to friends and mentors about toxic tendencies. We also must unlearn unhealthy patterns of behavior and remember that we must stay in tune and connected with God who is our Soul Source. He will reveal internal issues to us.

A TALE OF TWO CITIES

⁂

When we discovered that I was pregnant again, Mr. Cain called our priest and revealed to him that we were expecting a child and needed to get married. My momma told him that if we were not married then our baby would not carry his last name and would be a "Thorpe". I was in love with him and believed he had good intentions. He was far from perfect, but he loved me in the way he knew how. Remember: hurt people, hurt people.

Our marriage started out rocky because my husband was having extramarital relations with other women. His mistresses would call our home phone and then hang up when I answered. From the beginning of our relationship until the end, other women were having his children and by the time I was 26 years old, I had three children and was in a terrible marriage. I struggled with this reality because he was never home. He was a hard worker and an excellent provider, but he dishonored our union by being a whore and an abusive husband. I think he wanted to be a better man, but because of his upbringing and surroundings, he was not equipped with the necessary tools.

We were young, and this was the first marriage for both of us. He wove a major web of destruction by producing so many children with other women during our marriage, and it was too much to bear. I felt like a fool and looked like one too. Some women who were gossiping about me were going through the same situation or worse, behind the thick drapery that veiled their misery. They didn't leave their partners either.

I distinctly remember the day I finally gained the courage to separate from my husband. It was a cold winter evening around 4:30 p.m. The night before, he had worked a long shift and was resting comfortably in our warm home. Something shifted within me and it felt as if I had suddenly regained my senses. While he dozed off, I took the keys to his truck, searched the vehicle for proof of his many indiscretions and found exactly what I was looking for. I discovered a letter written by a woman to help defend him in court against another woman who he allegedly fathered four children with. Mr. Cain was the biological father of her three oldest children.

Oh, the tangled webs we weave when we first practice to deceive! I woke my husband from his slumber and showed him the letter. He was in disbelief. He looked confused as his new reality began staring him in the face. He angrily threw my house keys into the open field next to our home. That would be the last time he had an opportunity to toss my keys to keep me under his control.

In that moment, I had a flashback to the knock on the door we received when the sheriff served papers for his illegitimate children. I was in total shock upon seeing the long list of names of children that my husband fathered while we were married. I was a young woman in love with an abusive man who was also a Casanova and it does not get any worse than that. I was adrift in the body of a young woman who lost her self-esteem, self-dignity, and self-identity because of the pain of emotional and physical abuse. I asked myself, " *Where do I go from here?* "

I grew up in the Catholic church and believed that divorce was a sin, and therefore, it was not an option. I was not attending church regularly and I didn't have a strong relationship with the Lord. I only called on Him during the bad times. I neglected my spiritual relationship with Him when things were going well which was a cycle that continued for a while. As more pain was inflicted, I called on Him to help me in my time of need. When things got better, I would take the licks and keep on ticking. I thanked God for His mercy and then viewed Him as an afterthought when the seas were smooth. I could not fathom divorcing my husband and felt as if I were trapped. I developed a mindset that made me defensive and unwilling to relinquish my husband or let other women ruin my home.

Let's talk about mentality and frame of mind for just a moment. I had a simple-minded mentality because of limited education and sheltered perspectives. For once, I listened to the voice in my head telling me I deserved better. As a woman, I had the foresight to consider the possibility of a day coming when his children would search for their father. I believed they deserved to be a part of their father's life, and I also knew I was not a woman who could handle that. He became more mean-spirited and vindictive towards me as a new life emerged. He was the only man in my life between the ages of fifteen to twenty-six. I knew I was ready to explore the world on my own and live for my kids, but I had one problem that I did not realize would leave me bankrupt and having to start over. My husband had the money, and money was power that he used to his advantage. I knew there were other women who would request and be granted child support and I wanted to make sure that each of my children were taken care of.

Our family court judge favored the children conceived within marriage over the children conceived because of infidelity. My ex-husband was ordered to pay quite a bit of child support to me, plus alimony. This was the only way for me to rebuild my life, but he did not make it easy for me. The judge temporarily granted me the possession of our newer vehicle, but Mr. Cain fought and regained possession of the car for a while, but only until the final order was issued that granted me ownership of the Volvo. Our divorce caused what many refer to as "bad blood," and there was a lot of it. Let's just say that he and his friends made sure that when I got the car back it was completely run down and would cost a small fortune to repair.

My momma planted an image in mind that made me view my father as a good man, but I found out that he was not all he appeared to be. Both of the men in my life, who I gave my heart to, let me down. Life teaches us lessons and we learn through the ups and downs and the twists and turns. After returning home from college, getting pregnant, and marrying the one I thought would be the love of my life, our hearts were shattered. There were good times, as in any relationship, but the bad times outweighed them. Momma advised me to leave if the bad outweighed the good.

Each time I got pregnant, there were other women bringing precious life into the world. He brought those children into the world with a scarlet letter on their chests. They did not ask or choose the circumstances surrounding their births. It is not fair to an innocent child who had nothing to do with being born to be talked down upon or mistreated. When I was only twenty-one years old and not equipped to deal with such hurt and pain, I found myself angry at the women. I took my marriage vows seriously and wanted to believe my husband when he told me he did not father those kids. His mouth said one thing and my eyes told me something totally different. I remember picking up my daughter from school and noticing this pretty little girl who was staring me in my eyes. I thought that she favored my husband and when I confronted him about the girl's resemblance to him, he said she was not his child.

Because of Mr. Cain's deceitful involvement in the night life and being out in the streets, he became verbally abusive and called me names I was not accustomed to hearing. He called me a "bitch" or a "whore", which infuriated me. I had never even been with another man and felt disrespected and deeply hurt by his outbursts. The emotional abuse hurt me to the core of my being. My momma raised me with integrity and high moral standards. I was Daddy's little princess who thought I found my prince. He turned out to be everything except my expectation.

One night after we argued, he pushed me out of the house, took the baby, and locked the door. It was an extremely cold winter night and he left me outside shivering wearing only a short night gown and my undergarments. After the initial shock dissipated, I looked up and saw him looking through the window with our child in his arms, callously taunting me. We had weekly arguments that escalated into violence. By this time, I had enough of the abuse and I snapped. I went into the glove compartment of his truck and took out his revolver. He could see what I was doing, so he came to the carport and began moving his hands frantically while saying, "No, it has bullets!" All I remember is pointing the gun at him and I heard my neighbor, "No Dina! Don't do it! He ain't worth it!" I cried profusely and screamed, "I am tired of him hitting me!" I fired the .38 revolver and realized that the gun was fully loaded.

By the grace of God, Mr. Cain ducked. If he had not made that split-second decision, there would have been a vastly different ending to both my story and his. I thank God for sparing both of our lives that day. I never intended to kill him, but I wanted him to know I was tired and no longer afraid of him. I cannot count the times I called the police to rescue me during our tumultuous marriage. They knew me by name.

Rattled after this close call, I headed to my momma's home and I passed a police officer on the way. I signaled to him that I needed help and when he approached me I told him I had just shot at my husband. He paused for a moment and then asked if my husband was still alive. He walked to my car, retrieved the gun, removed the bullets and returned the gun to me. He instructed me to head on over to my momma's house. When I arrived, I told her what happened and handed her the gun.

Over the years, Mr. Cain asked my momma to return his gun and she always responded, "No sir! So you can kill my daughter?" Momma held onto the gun for over a decade until my bonus dad gave it back to him. No one believed I would ever leave Mr. Cain because I kept going back to him and repeating the same pattern of abuse. My momma was exhausted and was ready to handle the situation on her own terms. I went to a safe shelter for counseling and lived there for a brief period of time, but I left before my counseling was complete. Because of my circumstances, I went back to Mr. Cain.

My brothers were tired of seeing me suffer. My younger brother was constantly coming to my home to help me take my clothing and put them into trash bags when I promised I was leaving Mr. Cain. I would escape temporarily and then return. One of my brothers remarked, "All Mr. Cain has to do is rub Dina's behind and she goes right back to him." My dad did not really know the extent of the abuse I dealt with. Despite the agony I endured, I still wanted to keep my abuser safe. I remember looking in the mirror one day and cutting my hair short. I had a hard time believing that the woman in the mirror was really me. Being slapped at nine months pregnant is traumatizing to both the mother and child. My babies and I were on the receiving end of abuse during every pregnancy.

At one point, my six-year-old daughter pulled a butcher knife on her father as he started to beat me in the kitchen. She jumped between us to protect me and he thought it was funny. We were both exposing this child to violence at such a young age. My focus was to get my kids out of that situation and the one thing I felt I did right was to finally leave.

Mr. Cain had another woman from his past that I rightfully assumed was still a part of his life. I remember my cousin telling me, "Mr. Cain was in the projects with this woman who kept a nasty house." This mistress would mother several of his children during our marriage. One night, he left the house and went to a club near our home. When he returned, everything appeared to be fine until he woke up the next morning and discovered that the tires on three of our four vehicles were slashed! Our newest car was parked close to the doorway of our house and was the only one that did not sustain damage. I was completely shocked and confused. He told me he knew who did it.

Apparently, there was a confrontation between him and another woman at the club the night before. She was upset because

WHEN THE CURTAIN FALLS

he would not acknowledge their children or provide them with any form of support. I learned about these details in retrospect because of Ms. Unapologetic sending papers to our house that let me know she had children with him. My best friend worked with her at a restaurant in town. Ms. Unapologetic befriended her to find out more information about my relationship with my husband. Through the rumor mill, my momma found out that Ms. Unapologetic was planning to bring her children to my doorstep to confront their father. Well, let us just say that I was a noticeably quiet woman in those days. This woman DID NOT want to bring her children to my home because when it came to dealing with other women who were trying to steal my husband, I was never afraid. Case and point: Mr. Cain was supposed to take our daughters trick-or-treating one year when our children were younger. Instead of walking the neighborhood and spending quality time with our girls while they collected candy, he used one of our vehicles to pick up a random woman he was cheating on me with.

To his surprise, I happened to be out running an errand and noticed them in the car next to me at a red light. When I innocently turned my head to look around while I waited for the light to change, my unintentional glance quickly turned into rage. I got out of my car and started beating on the window of their vehicle. I was pregnant with our third daughter and felt completely powerless. He turned down a street to escape my fury. Unbeknownst to me, students from the school that I taught at were watching the entire altercation in real-time. I did not even notice them because I was too focused on trying to figure out who this strange woman was in my husband's truck. As I pounded the window and yelled at them, she sat frozen in the vehicle and did not move a muscle. As I screamed at my husband to explain himself, she sat in the passenger seat of his truck with the door locked.

She did not move as me and Mr. Cain argued. My main objective was to get her out of the truck. I will admit that my anger was misguided. I was married to my husband, not her. If I was going to act a fool, it should have been with him first. At one point, Mr. Cain got out of his vehicle to attempt to restrain me. Frightened and overcome with guilt, she used this opportunity to speed off in his vehicle. After we finished arguing in the street, I drove to his mother's house. I was very upset and crying profusely. His mother was as tired of our drama as mine was by now. Here I stood, six months pregnant with our third child, and he was embarrassing her by carrying on in the way that he had grown accustomed. I was hysterical and the only thing I remember is that his mother got into her car and told me she would be back shortly. She came to my defense that night by being truly disappointed in her son and the way he lived his life.

Looking back at the situation, I cannot help but think of all the people who tried to come to my aid and assist me in navigating this uncharted territory. Because of my husband's many extramarital relationships, I unwittingly contracted sexually transmitted diseases. I reluctantly found myself in and out of doctor's offices repeatedly because of his repulsive lifestyle. I found it strange that he would almost boast about the fact that many men would not tell their partners the truth and lie to them about how they contracted an STD. He would just tell me, "You need to go to the doctor." When I look back, I question what kind of person would repeatedly do this to someone they were supposed to love. Alas, a wounded person who has no direction would, and did, cause this type of harm to me on multiple occasions. I thought I was living in a horror story.

I was hiding behind the curtains covering my shame and I could not share this part of my life with anyone. I was simply too embarrassed. The first time I contracted a venereal disease early in my marriage, I was in denial. I knew I was being faithful to my husband, and I assumed there was no way on Earth this could happen to me. I am blessed to say that I am HIV negative. When visiting these doctors, I was always so embarrassed. The doctors would look at me and say, "You're such a beautiful young woman..." with a baffled look on their faces. They could not understand how I arrived in such precarious situations. I bounced around from doctor to doctor to hide my shame behind the curtains that I installed in the windows of my life. I could not let the drapery fall and expose all my faults. Yet, domestic violence has no face.

Mr. Cain was a charmer, and he always knew what to do to get me back into his good graces. I loved receiving nice gifts, and he would cry and tell me how sorry he was. As a master manipulator, he knew what to do to convince me to take him back. I do believe that some small part of him was genuinely apologetic for his actions, but he had a problem that he was unwilling to admit to himself. He was even more unwilling to help resolve my issues. This vicious cycle would reprise itself to haunt me in years to come. I advise people to be careful how they treat others and to withhold their judgment, because we cannot always know the full details of the depth of someone else's story. I now know why my level of anxiety was heightened. I had endured traumatic stress in so many areas of my life. While living through this nightmare, I did not realize or understand how close God was to me. He was an ever-present help in my time of need. I now recognize this protection as His grace and mercy. Because of His unceasing love, I can declare that I have never been hospitalized or thought of committing suicide despite the struggles I faced.

I had to be courageous, and find my God-given strength to stay in a relationship like my marriage. I had to make sure my plan of action could be executed perfectly so that I would remain alive. He once told me, "If you leave me, I will kill you." I often thought I would die at the hands of a man, but my exit plan was organized and ready to be carried out. Unknowingly, I had my Heavenly Father walking by my side every step of the way. The Lord stood by me and strengthened me so that, through my testimony, His message might be fully proclaimed and all the Gentiles would hear. I was rescued from the lion's mouth. In Timothy 4:17, Timothy's mentor was in jail and his church was in turmoil. He was not feeling brave, but Paul subtly told him that God was calling him to preach. He told Timothy that the Lord will give us the courage to do what He has called us to do. In that very moment, God was giving me the courage and strength to escape from my toxic relationship and get a glimpse of my future life. It takes a lot of grape crushing to produce fine wine. God was going to give me what I needed to accomplish what He had commanded me to do, and I would have to finally walk by faith and not by sight. It was time to put in the work required to fulfill my destiny.

Our divorce was a bitter one, and he was angry that he no longer had me around to be his human punching bag. He did not want to pay child support and had the best legal counsel in the city of Savannah. Despite Mr. Cain's power over me, I believed that God would come to my aide. I finally left and never looked back. I got my tubes tied because I knew I had enough children after my third child was born. I left when she was ten months old. My momma told me to only have as many children as I could take care of. I did not want to be single, but I had no choice. I had to show my children an example of a strong woman and I didn't want them to think it was okay for a woman to be beaten. As a young woman, I learned many valuable lessons such as, it is important to get to know a man before becoming his girlfriend. Learn about his family and friends, do not engage in premarital sex, listen to those who have wisdom, and never give up on yourself because God has not forgotten you. In my heart, mind, body, and soul I longed for peace. God was waiting to give it to me when I was ready to receive it. I needed to seek counseling again because domestic violence is a life-altering event. Fear ruled my mind and trickled into all areas of my life.

Growth 101 – Don't be afraid to reach out to support the person you feel is being abused. Don't allow a perfect opportunity to assist leave you silent; it may be their last hope for life. Remember, life is extremely lonely for someone being abused; they are holding in a lot because of fear of their abuser. It is important not to judge others. Abusers can be truly kind and, in many cases, remorseful. They are damaged people who need help.

FOLDED IN THE CURTAINS

❧

In the beginning, I wanted to hide behind the many curtains hanging around me. I wanted my life to be a total secret. I cared too much about my image and keeping up with the status quo. One of the biggest issues I faced was wanting to be something that I was not. This was undoubtedly a flaw in my character. People within the community oftentimes already knew what was going on within my marriage. I was the last to find out. The "street committee" was gossiping about what should have been private matters between me and my husband.

The women he was involved with had friends who mentioned his proclivities to their friends, and then their friends had other connections to those who knew the involved parties. Everybody talked and gossiped. Trying to put the pieces of my life back together was an arduous task. Despite our imperfections, my daughters were fortunate to have the opportunities that other children with two-parent households were afforded. I put them in ballet classes, they played basketball, they learned to play instruments, and they were able to attend youth organizations in Savannah. I

exposed them to the same activities and interests I had as a child. One of my daughters was nominated as Best Camper and was rewarded with an opportunity to attend the 1996 Olympic Games that were hosted in Atlanta, Georgia.

When my girls were young, I was able to get assistance for day-care services due to my income. I actively sought out and took advantage of every positive opportunity that was available to us. I was in contact with a number of people who saw something promising within me and wanted to assist me in rebuilding my life. At the beginning of my separation/divorce, my ex-husband would not assist with any of the girls' needs and he rarely played an active role in their lives. In order to receive child support for our kids, I had to file a child support petition with the court. Throughout every blow that was handed to me during our battle, I kept fighting for and taking care of my daughters.

What I discovered was that when God is working in your favor, He comes to your aid in your time of need. I always knew I loved the Lord, but I did not have a personal relationship with Him. There were times I recall being so angry with my circumstances I would say, "God, I hate you!" Of course, I would always take it back because I knew that even on my worst days He was there in the midst of the chaos. When I look back, I feel terrible that I uttered those words, but that was how I expressed my anger -- through swearing. I continued to push forward with the tools I had gained at this stage in my journey, and fortunately, help was on the way! At least for my professional life. I was a great paraprofessional, and I always kept my personal life separate from my professional life.

My ability to separate the two provided me with a new opportunity. The principal I was working under saw potential in me, and wrote a letter of recommendation for me when I applied to Dewitt Wallace Reader's Digest Pathways to Teaching Program. There was a selection process and I was accepted into a minority teaching program to recruit highly qualified minority teachers into the program. This is when my life turned around. I vowed to work hard to get this degree, no matter the cost. This aspiration proved to be exceedingly difficult. When they were not scheduled to work at their own jobs, my momma and brother assisted with watching my daughters for me. Sometimes I had to take my girls to class with me. The janitors would watch them while I attended lectures, or my professors would allow them to sit in their office during class. My daughters were well-mannered and studious. They used that time to complete their homework assignments and entertain each other. I checked on them periodically and the janitors would peek into my classes through the door's window and gesture to me that they were fine.

I continued to work as a paraprofessional in the daytime and attended night classes until I needed to take certain courses that were only taught during morning hours. At that point in my education, I took a leave of absence from work so that I could complete my course of study. I promised myself that once I got my bachelor's degree, I would re-enroll my daughters into private school. I wanted to provide them with the same opportunity that my parents gave me.

My education was built on strong religious and academic teaching, which would later take me back to my Southern Baptist roots. I earned my bachelor's degree in English from Savannah State University in 1998. Afterward, I began working on my first teaching certification in middle school English and History. I passed the examination on my first attempt! I always knew God had bigger plans for my life, but first I had to believe I could do it. To quote Heb. 11:1 (KJV), "Now faith is the substance of things hoped for and the evidence of things not seen." Like a young child who becomes anxious while eagerly anticipating a special gift, I too had to believe, through faith, that God was going to fulfill his promise.

Even though my confidence had been stripped away, I needed to wholeheartedly trust that I would one day become a teacher. Each time I moved forward in my career or within my educational pursuits, I was so proud of myself. I never forgot that I had battled back from the pits of hell to make it to that point. I was intrinsically motivated to help other women avoid the same pitfalls that I had succumbed to, but first I needed to be healed from those wounds. I got a taste of academic and professional success, so I got my master's in education while working at an alternative school as a permanent substitute teacher. My desire to become an exceptional children's instructor was sparked while at the alternative school. I got a special education certification concurrent with my master's degree. After becoming burned out while teaching at the alternative school, I decided I needed a change. I accepted a position at a local high school where I remained for thirteen and a half years. I used this time to work on tier one of my doctorate degree.

I enjoyed my new work environment and even though I had a lot of obstacles to overcome, I was extremely driven and wanted to help the African American students who needed me. Immediately upon arriving on campus I knew exactly why God placed me there. I did my best to help as much as possible, but the African American males who always appeared to be misunderstood and handled differently pulled at my heartstrings. I intervened in any and every situation that I thought I could de-escalate. I didn't realize who my real boss was, but after years of dedication, it was revealed who truly represented the blood in the workforce. The sun was beginning to shine through the curtains.

I enjoyed looking at beautiful homes that rested on the entrancing streets of immaculate neighborhoods that had both charm and character. My brother knew this about me, and one day he invited me to go for a drive to look at houses. I told the realtor that I absolutely loved the homes, but they were beyond my reach. He understood and was undeterred. He took us to view several homes in a nearby neighborhood that may have been more attainable. I was extremely excited!

A few days after we perused those nice homes, I could not stop thinking about them and envisioning myself living happily within the walls of a beautiful home with my daughters. I spoke to my cousin who lived in the area and she instructed me to get in contact with her realtor. She wanted me to see if he could provide me with additional assistance. Her realtor connection was well-known in the Savannah area. He took me to a new development on the outskirts of town that had just entered a new phase of expansion. While he showed me the land, for the first time I heard God speak to me. He told me I was looking at my future home-site. I thought to myself, "No way! I can't purchase a home"! My first house was not in a good location and I sold it because my momma feared for my life. I couldn't move into the same area. I wanted to trust God, but I simply didn't know how. I began seeking His divine wisdom more. As I grew closer to my Heavenly Father, He revealed to me the passing of my beloved brother. I began having visions and glimpses into the future from this point on.

I purchased a home in 2009 and although I felt truly accomplished, I was still in a failing relationship with a man who proved to be unworthy of my love. I found myself once again needing an exit plan to save my life. My brother took his last breath in 2010. Through his passing, I got a glimpse of heaven and examined my own mortality in a totally different light. There was such a profound peace surrounding him as he made his transition and I am forever indebted to God for allowing me to witness this event. I made a covenant with God to be a more obedient Christian and although I did not change overnight, I gradually made serious changes regarding my faith.

I was indeed reborn and began asking myself, "When will I tell God thank you? When will I make time for God?" I began thinking about ways to walk closer with him and as I sought Him, my gifts and talents shifted. I felt as though someone else was directing my life. Before this revolution, I considered myself to be spiritually bankrupt. I lacked patience, wisdom, obedience, discernment, faith, confidence, forgiveness, and I had a judgmental spirit. I thank God for answering my prayer and revealing to me my faults. I needed to see and understand my flaws because I would always strive for perfection, but I learned that God is the only perfect being. I looked at life differently and began waiting on God. I studied the bible, meditated, sought counseling with my pastor, took profanity out of my vocabulary, and saturated my mind with the content found within spiritual books. All my other accolades no longer held the same value. I realized that growth was a powerful weapon. There was something burning inside of me that God wanted to shine brightly, but first I had to discover the gifts within me that were beginning to manifest.

Fast forward a bit to 2016. The school year was ending, and for the first time, I was feeling unfulfilled and unchallenged. I knew God had more planned for my life. The Lord instructed me to put myself out there and apply for different opportunities. He told me to take back my possessions, so I heeded his word and began by reclaiming my refrigerator and other large items from the school. Over the summer, I had four interviews for jobs that I believed would be a better fit for me. One opening was for an assistant principal position, and sadly I did not get the offer. As I prayed about it, I heard God tell me, "It is not over. You will get a call tomorrow." Just as He said, the next day I received a phone call and a job offer that I gladly accepted.

I trusted God and could see that he was expanding my territory while simultaneously blowing my mind with his faithfulness. I was actively seeking him and doing my best to be a faithful servant. As I continued to thirst for the things of Christ, I wanted to be more receptive to God and learn how to become a servant leader. I was actively involved in my church and volunteered with various activities. I spearheaded outreach programs for those affected by domestic violence and homelessness. This involvement gave me a feeling of sheer pleasure and fulfillment by assisting those who were in need. I listened attentively to my pastor's sermons as he both preached and poured knowledge into me. I converted three years prior because my spiritual needs were not being met by Catholicism. A priest who I was fond of violated the trust of one of my daughters and myself, which was another breach that left me feeling disappointed. More than ever, this made me feel as if I was just going through the motions at that church and not growing as a Christian. It was time to make a change, which encouraged me to attend the Baptist church that my beloved momma and Bonus Dad were attending.

For the first time in my life, I felt something powerful wash over me as I had an encounter with the Holy Spirit. As I began attending church more regularly and felt God leading me to be closer to my momma. I stared searchingly into my mirror, not to reflect on my beautiful exterior, but to peer within myself and ask God to reveal my faults to me. I lived about forty-five minutes away from her and would not see her as much as I wanted to. My encounter with a greater power, paired with my blossoming relationship with God, allowed me to grow closer to my momma. It is strange how God will sometimes bring families closer through religion. I started purchasing daily devotionals, bibles, and religious material. Any time I entered a store, I gravitated toward anything spiritual. I was excited about my faith and consumed with reading religious material. In retrospect, I see how God's plan was unfolding before it ever manifested in my life.

I was a very reserved person who was accustomed to the repetition of Catholicism. Once I began worshiping in a Baptist church, I received Christ in my life and became a born-again Christian. My life continued to flourish, both religiously and professionally, and I knew that was because of my obedience. Still, God wanted so much more from me. He was becoming my true love, but I still faced many tests and trials within my personal and professional life. I embraced this period of self-discovery, purpose, and exploring my God-ordained destination. I recognized who I was and to whom my life belonged. I had forgotten how to live a satisfying life. I was trying to save my daughters from succumbing to the statistics that stated they would not make it due to having been mothered by a nineteen-year-old. Because of our circumstances, I had to be their everything. My ex-husband rarely showed the girls love or attended any of their school functions or events. I had to be the breadwinner and I was trying my best to fill the shoes of both parental roles. My life was comprised of working hard during the days and being there for my girls each night. I masked my pain by letting myself become consumed with my career. In my mind, I was determined to prove to my ex-husband that I could make it on my own and thrive by being all the things he told me I was not. To hide the misery of the failed relationship with my first love, I hid behind the curtains of my children and career. I was planning to never be intimate with another man for the rest of my life. I took my wedding vows seriously, but little did I know this journey would lead me straight toward my destiny.

My daughters were all grown up and started living their own lives. They were all successful, according to man's standards. I had time to myself and a quietness that allowed me to hear that inner voice of God. He was trying to guide me along by pushing me to do more and trust that He would grant me the ability to fulfill His calling. He revealed bits and pieces at a time about what I would soon experience. I did not understand what He was doing. Now I see He was preparing me for a greater purpose. John 16:21 (NASB) reads, "Whenever a woman has labor, she has pain, because her hour has come; but when she gives birth to the child, she no longer remembers the anguish because of the joy that a child has been born in the world." I was experiencing growth in a way that I never imagined was possible for me and that I felt I could only dream about.

I found myself drawn to Facebook, which I thought was odd considering that I never wanted people in my business. I held onto

WHEN THE CURTAIN FALLS

what little comfort I could muster by hiding behind the curtains that encapsulated my world. I felt as if my steps were being ordered by a higher power, and I was obedient to heed the calling on my life. I started reconnecting with old friends and I was super excited! I found a very special friend, Cheryl Polote-Williamson, and I started following her on different social media platforms. We both grew up in Savannah and met in high school. We formed a bond that would last decades. I was truly inspired by her posts and extremely excited to find out she was a published author. I shared her posts to encourage others and support her throughout her endeavors. I did not know that one day she would provide me with an opportunity to be a part of *Soul Source,* which is a book that became a best-selling award winner. This project changed my life forever. It helped catapult the process of my restoration and healing. At first, I wondered to myself, "How could sharing a portion of my story be powerful?" The key word here is "portion". There was so much more that had not been revealed. The anguish of surviving molestation, rape, domestic violence, failed relationships, and deceit left my daughters and me emotionally wounded. Because I finally faced my pain head-on, we could move forward within the grace of God. To reach this point, I had to let go of some things that weighed me down.

Growth 101 - I had to ask myself tough questions such as: How do I forgive people? How do I forgive the errors of my ways? What does forgiveness even look like in this situation? What does forgiveness feel like? Is it passive? Is it aggressive? Who needs to receive it? Who wants to receive it? Who deserves it? How many times am

71

I expected to forgive? Is it my responsibility to forgive someone who has caused me harm? If I harm someone, do I ask for forgiveness? What will it cost me to forgive? Is forgiveness an agreement? Should I live with unforgiveness forever? If I choose to live with unforgiveness forever, what would that do to my heart? If I live with unforgiveness, what does that burden do to my soul? If I live with unforgiveness, what does it do to my spirit? Should I always forgive? Do I extend forgiveness to some and not to others? Is forgiveness truly for me? Who can benefit from forgiveness? Is the world I live in a forgiving world? Is forgiveness just for family members? Should I forgive a stranger on the street? What is the unforgivable sin? Is there an unforgivable sin?

I found my mind racing because I wanted to please God so badly. I could not escape Him or the Holy Spirit speaking to me. As a blind person can sometimes see shapes and try to identify objects, I too had blind spots that needed to be brought into focus. I wanted my life to be a testimony that allowed others to see my transparency and truth. I needed to pull back the curtains which were hiding my shame and expose my story so that others could find their way in Christ. Imagine the sweet naïve Catholic girl turning into a Baptist! Proverbs 3:5 tells us to, "Trust in the Lord with all your heart and lean not on your own understanding." I had to trust that God was leading me toward a greater calling and grant myself the mercy to let the curtains surrounding me fall to the wayside.

I needed to bring up parts of my life that were filled with bitterness toward other women who harmed me. I thought I had released them from my burden, but upon taking forgiveness classes I realized I had not. Isaiah 26:3 (KJV) states, "Thou wilt keep him in perfect peace, whose mind is stayed on thee, because he trusts thee. Trust ye in the Lord forever, for in the Lord Jehovah is everlasting strength." I realized that I absolutely must trust God during this process as I accepted that the curtains surrounding me needed to be withdrawn to let His light shine through. God wanted to use me as a vessel to help others forgive. He taught me to accept my past experiences for what they were and use those weak moments to help other people through learning how to forgive—no matter the amount of pain and no matter the offense.

DOUBLE LAYERED CURTAIN INTERTWINED WITH CAREER AND LOVE

❧

I was being transformed through a preordained spiritual shift so that I could reach a higher level of fulfillment. I needed to understand how tests would manifest and how to overcome the trials and tribulations attached to growing. Victory often requires patience and faith. Through living a life of obedience to God, walls around my life were tumbling just like the walls of Jericho. God made it very plain that I could not be in a sexual relationship with a man. I needed to go through a tough test to reach the other side of my Jordan River. I knew there would be tough times, but I believed it was worth it to follow God's plan for my life because deliverance was on the way.

In Mark 9:23 (KJV), "Jesus said unto him, If thou canst believe, all things are possible to him that believeth". I needed to believe this. I had to learn to unleash my truth by making a mental shift, which proved to be a painful challenge because of my belief systems and the generational patterns that needed to be broken. I knew that education was not the only gift that God bestowed upon me. I was ready to move in a different direction. I started searching my soul so that I could finally be true to myself. God was repositioning me and making me uncomfortable so that I would eventually accept that change was necessary to move forward.

As I grew as a woman of God, I could see how he was tailor-making me. I needed to learn how to sit in silence and cast all my cares and anxieties upon Him. I allowed my heart to speak to God because I longed for a deeper relationship with the Father. I regularly cried out to Him and told Him my inner thoughts, asking Him to show me how to speak to Him. I wrote out several ways that I could be in His presence. This allowed me to become an out-of-the-box thinker.

Growth 101- I began speaking to God by reading Him the list I made of ways to enter his presence. I read it as if He were in the room. I became still and silently waited to hear God speak. There were several occasions when He made it very plain what I should do and provided me with the strategy. I longed to find peace and knew God was the answer. My love life and career were two areas that needed change. I needed to know whose I was and who was my real boss.

I have a genuine love for children and at an incredibly young age, I knew teaching was something that I wanted to do. In 1986, I began my career in education and have over 30 years of dedicated service to one school district. Over my career, I have worked 6 ½ years as a paraprofessional and 22 years as a teacher with the Department of Specialized Instruction. I have a Bachelor of Arts degree in English Language and Literature and I hold middle school, special education, and leadership certification. I have a genuine love for the artform of instructing and enjoy the opportunity to transfer what I have learned to the students who benefit from my wisdom and guidance.

Through years of hard work and dedication, I achieved a position as a Center Leader, the equivalent of a Principal in an alternative setting. I have worked on the elementary, middle, and high school levels, taught English in middle school, been a co-teacher for elementary and high school-aged children, served as a Resource Teacher for the Exceptional Children's Department, and spent some time as an EIP teacher.

Teaching allowed me to accept the sunlight that had begun to shine through the drapery which was covering my truth. I saw how hard work paid off and how the end-game resulted in the greatest lesson, test, and testimony of my life. Based on my first-hand struggles with self-esteem and fear throughout my educational pursuits, I used my insight to propel my students to achieve higher levels and helped shape many young minds throughout my career. God gave me the ability to care for the students and love them just as I loved my own children. They knew I valued them, which always made my job easier. The more defiant students posed a greater challenge, behaviorally speaking, but they were typically my favorites. I loved the challenge of trying to help the students in my program, but was often overwhelmed because of a lack of adequate resources being channeled to the areas that needed the funding. I was not shy in expressing my concerns over a lack of funding and developed my spiritual muscles for the battles to come. I did not envision my fight being lost, but what was ahead would prove to be what would propel me forward into my God-given purpose. It was important that I study my craft so that I could continue to support my student's growth and development. Who knew that my personal life would become intertwined with my career and give me a chance to learn amazing lessons.

My rise to the top was accompanied by the falling of old, tattered curtains falling around me. Beware of people who envy your gifts and talents. They see your potential and feel threatened, while others will try to keep you in a certain place for their benefit. There are backstabbers who appear to like you, but once you turn your back they talk negatively about you, and don't forget the naysayers who wear a smile but carry a knife behind their back. In the end, each of these characters serve a purpose and will help you grow, so I would like to thank each person who played such a role in my life. Today, I salute you for being a part of my greatness.

Growth 101 - Growth is painful.

Why would I salute those who persecuted me? I did it because it was a part of God's great plan for my life. I needed to grow and I trusted the process. There may have been moments when it was uncomfortable, but I can still tell my story and show you God's glory. When I left the education field, I had made my mark but left feeling unappreciated and unloved by a system that I gave a large portion of my life and sacrificed many weekends to.

For example, the Alternative Assessment portfolio was a program used to assess students identified as having significant cognitive disabilities and even with maximum accommodation cannot participate in the general assessment program. The parent of one student wanted them in the general education population instead, and that was within her rights. The Alternative Assessment portfolio needed to be conducted in an Inclusion setting since the student being served was using the Inclusion model of instruction. None of the general education teachers could get the student to do any work, so as the case-manager, it was my responsibility to complete the task. The student was an autistic student which made it even more challenging, but after advocating for myself, I was given additional time to complete the portfolio. I had to do the work as a special education teacher in a separate room, which is why the portfolio did not pass. One teacher suggested that, in order to get a passing score, I should simply say that I did it in Inclusion, but I stuck to my principles, morals, and integrity as an educator.

I began advocating for the teachers and the future teachers who had to complete this program and even though my efforts and courage was applauded by one of my superiors, she warned me that advocating for the teachers would come with a price. It was a price that I was willing to pay to help future teachers who had to complete this portfolio.

There was a system in place, but it did not offer adequate training, support or resources to assist the teachers in being successful—I was told to "just make it happen." This was a major problem which was reflected by the district's scores. This was so unfair to the teachers and the students and what should have been a win-win for all, was instead a losing situation. The students in my Inclusion classes suffered severely that year. I was rarely in the class, and for months at a time I worked through my entire weekend to complete the portfolio.

Another noteworthy moment in my career was when I was handpicked by district personnel to work with students. Teachers either didn't want to work above and beyond or just did not have the ability to provide the services. I knew God placed me at this school to assist students and that is what I did. I was known for being an innovative teacher. I was loved and respected by the parents of my students who knew that I had their back and the back of their child. Whatever it took, I was going to motivate them and improve both their academics and their behavior. I was a team player that wanted to see others win. I was afforded the opportunity to train teachers and paraprofessionals, which ultimately allowed me to be a department chair for the Exceptional Children's Department.

Later in my career, although I handled any task assigned to me, I often found myself being held accountable for situations that were just beyond my control. For many years I lived in chaotic en-

vironments so the one thing that I truly believed in was a condu-
cive learning environment. God needed to place me in this environment to prepare me to birth my own baby and produce radical
changes for the students. My philosophy has always been to treat
students with respect and treat them the way you wanted your
child to be treated. I wanted my students to become self-directed
learners and to take ownership of their learning environment. It
was my job to make sure students are learning and monitor their
progress on a daily basis. I asked myself tough questions to self-
evaluate myself as an educator because it was my goal to become
better than I was the day before. One of my greatest gifts was being
able to love all people and being a versatile educator and I prided
myself in being a humble servant. Just to name a few of my accolades: received race to the top bonus merit pay because of student
achievement; recognized as district teacher leader; Pathways to
Teaching Scholar; Teacher of the Year Nominee for 2000 and
2001; Paraprofessional of the Year; Phi Lambda Theta International Honor Society Member; opportunity to provide a Power-
Point presentation for Superintendent, board members and principals on the co-teaching model of instruction; and developed and
elicited various pamphlets to assist teachers in working with students with various learning disorders. Despite these accolades,
something was still missing in my life. Finding balance after so
much pain has always been a challenge for me and working like a
machine kept my mind off the pain and allowed me to feel as if I
was helping others. I found true gratification in helping others and

I always loved teaching, but in year twenty six, I was sad and disappointed by the way Inclusion was working in the district. This was one reason so many of my colleagues and I either applied for other jobs or left the school system.

To give you a little background on Inclusion, it's built on the premise that a student with special needs will have a greater advantage for success in life when there are more social interactions in a mixed environment. Yes, this can work if all involved are willing to see it succeed. Unless funding allocations are made available to allow more teachers per student the success will be minimal. Many teachers were tired, and because the school system is a system, you had to be careful about how you maneuvered. In other words, leave without giving the real reason you were leaving.

In the earlier part of my career, during the 2004 school term, I was afforded the opportunity to conduct a presentation, along with the general education teacher, before the professional senate, superintendent, board members, and principals. Inclusion was approved to be implemented the following year district-wide, but it was very disappointing to see Inclusion not work at optimal level. I watched Full Inclusion work for the first year while being supported and governed by a particular entity. This entity was able to monitor the success of both teachers and students to ensure all components were in place and used with fidelity. After the entity stopped training and eliciting strategies to both general education and co-teachers, the model was not working at its optimal level. The students were not being served properly and I could no longer tolerate that, which is why, after 13½ years at the same school, I shifted. Teachers were not being used as they were intended and I was in a place where I could not grow. I was unfulfilled and sensed there was something more God had for me to do.

I wanted a change and little did I know that God would use an acquaintance that I met while at Savannah State College, Mr. Spaulding. I met Mr. Spaulding in the early 1990's and can still remember that day and the location where we met. My car had stopped, and as I was standing outside my car, here comes my hero. He was a very tall, dark, and handsome young man with a beautiful smile, willing to give a helping hand. When he saw that my car would not start, he offered me a ride home. We had a great conversation and he gave me his number, but I was disappointed to find out later that he was married. When he called me I told him we couldn't talk anymore and we didn't see each other again until I saw him at an open house event at school. I saw Mr. Spaulding again at my church and my heart skipped a beat when he sat right behind me. I spoke, but that's all the words that would come out of my mouth. A feeling came over me that I can't explain and it's one that I would continue to ignore.

In 2015, I was dating Mr. Wolf who I met at a basketball tournament. I was working as a ticket taker and while on break I sat next to Mr. Wolf while in the eating area. He had a very charismatic personality which seemed to be a trait which I always seemed to be drawn to. We had something in common and continued to chit chat until my break was over. I didn't think much of it, but the school secretary told me that Mr. Wolf called and was eager to see me again. I was just getting out of a long-term relationship which, for many reasons, created pain so I was just as excited. He invited me to church, and the next day he sent two dozen roses to me at the school. I had never dated a man who had invited me to their church, so I thought this would be a great way to begin a relationship. Mr. Wolf offered me a key to his apartment, and even though I initially expressed my concern about staying there because we had just met, I eventually agreed.

It was a major mistake for me to take Mr. Wolf at face value and when I entered his apartment and saw that his clothes were in a box, I gave him the benefit of the doubt and assumed it was because he had just moved. He was handsome but I couldn't quite figure out why he looked so weathered. I enjoyed watching him coach and was flattered when he wanted me to attend all of his games. He professed his love and appreciation for me in front of the congregation at my church and when he invited me to go home with him for Christmas to meet his family, he was disappointed when I opted not to go because I thought it was just too soon. He traveled a lot and when he was away, he parked one of his trucks at my place. One day when I returned home, I noticed a particular odor. I know he smoked cigars, but this smelled like marijuana and I was extremely upset when he later admitted that he smoked marijuana. Not only was it illegal, he was putting his job on the line. I sounded like his mother when I lectured him and even though he appeared to be remorseful, his patterns changed. When I called him on the phone and I didn't get an answer, I thought something may have happened to him, so I rode up the road to check on him and was shocked to see beer and whiskey bottles everywhere. I learned a valuable lesson: What you see on the outside has nothing to do with what is happening on the inside. In his life and in my own life, the curtains had to fall. One day, out of the blue, he told me I was not the woman for him and if I wanted to be a part of the team I could be. That was a joke because there would be no team playing for me. Love will make you do crazy things as I fell into the same pattern, the same script, but a different actor.

I really needed a genuine friend in my life, and this is what Mr. Spaulding personified. He was no longer married, and was in a transitional relationship with someone he had been engaged to for over twelve years. She wanted to get married, but I believe he was afraid of failing again. When he told me I was the first woman he allowed to eat off of the china from his divorce, I knew he had not let go of his first wife, which was the real reason he could not commit. Our friendship was a genuine friendship with no sexual intimacy for a long duration until one day we both decided to cross the line and I questioned God when he revealed that he was supposed to be my husband or maybe it wasn't God speaking because I knew that "he already has a woman." I had to remember that God was going to work this situation out for my good—not to make me happy, but to fulfill his purpose. I had a different mindset and was trusting God, but I was also confused because Mr. Wolf was trying unsuccessfully to re-enter my life. I was in and out of relationships or going through the turmoil of the relationship, with no time to recover from the trauma it brings. I wanted to give love and be loved but was seeking it from men who were ill prepared and, most times, broken.

Growth 101 - As a woman, I needed to heal from one relationship before moving into another. This is crucial.

What I liked about Mr. Spaulding was the fact that he was honest, but I deserved more. I was convicted about our relationship because, first of all, I never intended to harm another woman and secondly, I also didn't want a man who cheated. After going back and forth for at least two years I gave him an ultimatum--it was either her or me.

I met another man that I dated briefly and he gave me everything and anything I wanted. He handed over his checkbook, keys to the house, and helped me financially. We had planned to get married and had purchased an almost $10,000 set of wedding rings. God let me know he was not the man for me and in order for me to get my husband, I must live a celibate life. Sometimes it takes making a mistake to get back on track and I realized my heart was still with the man who saved me as a damsel in distress over 30 years ago.

Growth 101 - Past mistakes and hurts: I felt my beauty was a curse that attracted darkness and because I lacked the power of discernment, I was drawn to it. I had to admit that I was hurt, I created hurt, and I needed to forgive myself for hurting other men. Through the pain of my failed relationships I turned around and did the same thing to men. God convicted me for my actions and upon self-reflection I realized I was working for man and not God. My greatest desire was to have a more intimate relationship with God so I needed to do things differently and apply the lessons learned to my life in order to live in his perfect will. I had to surrender all.

After the first book project, there was a new call on my life. I began soul searching and living a life of self-discovery. I asked myself whether I was living a self-directed life or a Christ-centered life. Was Christ on the throne or was I on the throne? I was learning, on my new journey, how to trust other women again after experiencing so much betrayal. My circles changed, and I met amazing women who were entrepreneurs with dreams and who were already on a journey to where I saw God was taking me. Collaboration is a key component that many women shy away from but it was time to let my light shine. I thought my purpose was to be an educator, but as I continued to do self-assessments, I realized that my purpose was not about education, degrees and material things, but it was about having a relationship with God and allowing him to be my primary focus.

I was a highly sought-after disciplinarian and did an outstanding job for a year while at this school. Now, with promotion comes a whole lot more jealousy, lies, and the enemy. I interviewed for an upper-level position and was called back for a second interview. The person that contacted me was someone I was not familiar with but was excited I received the call. There was something in my spirit about the person that was not sitting well. They seemed cold

-- almost like there was a hidden agenda. I would one day see that there was, indeed, a hidden agenda. I remember being grateful that God allowed me to stay one year at my new assignment. He revealed that I would not be there long based on the corruption that was taking place. I did like the fact that I was around a lot of women of color, but I did not like what took place behind the scenes. Their plan was to use me. They did not realize I had already done many of the assignments they were giving me and I had acted in the absence of the assistant principals. This left a sour taste in my mouth. After everything I had been through, they were not going to use me in my career or attempt to play me like a puppet or a fool. God was allowing me to speak up. Anytime I did not like something, I would speak out about it. I knew how to advocate for myself, and the one thing that people knew was not to mess with me. When I had enough, in many cases the harsh side of me would come out.

The assistant principals received compensation for Saturday school but wanted me to complete some of their paperwork and they receive compensation. An unfair workload was placed on me, but I could clearly see the underhandedness. I learned that sisterhood which was helping one another no matter what the cost. I was developing as a Christian woman and just did not like what I was seeing. I am far from being perfect, but I tried to conduct myself professionally, but one thing I know for sure these sisterhoods can be vindictive and calculating.

After one year, I was told by my Principal that the position was taken away because of the lack of progress and she had a position in the classroom, and she would love me to be an Inclusion teacher at her school. The same position I left due to it not working affectively and the feeling of not utilizing my gifts and talents. Meanwhile, I was only supposed to be at one school but ended up being split between two. The bottom line is there were women at the top using their power to their advantage and helping whoever they chose to help. I was now learning how the system worked and not liking what I was seeing. I was not about the game playing. I am a straight shooter and have no problems letting anyone know how I operate. I had no idea what I was getting myself into. I can remember being so excited about finally being promoted after many years of working hard.

My ability to stand up for myself was God maturing me for a much greater assignment, a calling. God called me to ministry and when I accepted the call, the warfare really began. I was working in a building that had so many issues I did not know where to begin or how to fix it all. I thought I could change what was broken, way before I got there, and I was used by a system that I loved. I would now be a scapegoat for what was unraveling way before my time. I just wanted to get from under such a person who said they represented one thing but just wanted to look good and not really be about the business of the children. I was given too many students who had true needs and not enough staff or resources to be effective.

Each life that I encountered was changed forever and I thank God for giving me the opportunity to change young lives. He gave me a brief assignment that would allow me to be the catalyst for change and change took place. I am forever grateful to be a part of a system where, even though man never truly rewarded me, God gave me the ultimate reward for my faithfulness to his children. I worked 28 years but was able to retire with 30 creditable years of teaching service. What was supposed to be my death was my resurrection. Resurrection is restoring the life which had ceased to exist, a setting up again, a giving back. Light is the natural agent that stimulates sight and makes things visible, and death is the opposite of life, a falling away from life. When we understand these terms, Christ's resurrection can be understood as the most momentous display of God's almighty power; one we, as man, should yearn for. My life felt much like a death after my divorce. Every area of my life was able to be resurrected. All curtains had fallen and I could now see the light. I was no longer hiding behind the curtain, no longer in a dead-end relationship, I was no longer going to church playing church, no longer sneaking and hiding thinking that no one saw me, I was no longer stuck in the past, and I had finally forgiven my family members for the wrong they did to me, including forgiving my father for leaving me at a time when I needed him.

I knew that my skills were beyond the classroom so when administration told me that I had to go back into the classroom, I began advocating for myself. The bottom line was, I had enough of the classroom and needed a break. I was ready to embark on the new. Somebody wanted me back in the classroom, but God was ready to work his miracle. I felt that God was showing a new and different light. I clicked on the computer and there was a position for a behavior specialist at an alternative school. I had worked on the high school level for most of my teaching career. I started in middle school and worked on the elementary level as a paraprofessional a few years as well. I knew the principal at the time and she was a little hesitant. It was a tough assignment, but my heart was in it.

The first thing I realized was the women were used to doing what they wanted to do. I was a new, self-taught behavior specialist and had always dealt with behaviors throughout my career and deserved the position, hands down. I was performing nine duties while supposedly the behavior specialist at this location. I was the RTI Coordinator, new teacher mentor liaison, P.E. teacher, behavior specialist, testing coordinator, medical liaison and coordinator for schools, Beacon coordinator, internship mentor go to, and professional development liaison. What I didn't know was that the school was underfunded and could not find certified teachers to work with the toughest elementary students in the school district.

These students were not able to perform in a regular setting due to behavior issues and were supposed to be a part of a 45-day or sometimes longer program. A newly elected principal was named because the other principal retired. A month before she retired, I received a phone call from upper management who told me I was going to get the position but if I opened my mouth I was going to be done! I talked to my momma about how she had talked to me and my momma revealed that someone had warned her about my boss. She is not to be trusted and once she finishes using you, she will discard you; and it came to pass. I remember a conversation with her about how I could not discuss the changing of leadership. She encouraged me and appeared to be happy to promote me. I was shocked at how fast it happened. Remember: all of this is new to me because I had never been trained to be an Assistant Principal, let alone a Principal. So, prior to my boss whom I also knew from growing up in my neighborhood said, "Redina this is your position." I am not equipped for this. I believe it was my position after all the hard work I put in the program, but he was good for the boys and they respected him, he was fair in his dealings with me and I loved working under him. I felt used by the two previous leaders, but I respected them and worked extremely hard to make them look good.

When the new principal announced that he was going to put me in the leadership program, my mind did not embrace it because I was ready to embark on the new. I told him this as well but, bless his heart, he wanted out. I was used as a pawn once again. I had a taste of the publishing world, speaker life, coaching life now this. The program started the end of September and he just wanted out which I believe that was the original plan but it wouldn't look right to just bring him back as a principal after having left the school system. I believe I made one or two meetings before the ball was dropped. He revealed he interviewed for a new position and thought he might get the job. I was excited for him and I was extremely loyal and supportive, so he advocated for me as well. He handed me the keys and walked out the door quicker than I had ever seen anybody leave. He handed me a failing program that needed to be cleaned up and who greater to do it. It was as if a weight had been lifted from his shoulders. I had no clue that I had just been handed my death sentence in the education arena.

I was extremely fatigued and exhausted from the last placement, and because we were always dealing with students with severe behavior problems, we never had time to do paperwork. For example, there might be three kids in the classroom and a teacher who was already let go was able to get back in the system. I would find myself having to be the principal and the behavior specialist. I asked a young man who was subbing if he was interested in working with these types of students. I had help from a veteran administrator who was well liked by the staff, but I didn't feel was strong as a disciplinarian. I felt the students needed more structure, but I was accused of not having any rules in place etc. and the team that supposedly had come to help me, was basically finding reasons I needed to be removed from the position. This was the absolute biggest favor I could have been given. The next year ten children were placed in the program and the bottom line is, my work had been completed. The program was exposed. I gave my heart and soul, and it was not good enough and I felt if I worked one more year my health would have taken a significant hit.

I was frustrated because I started the job cleaning up what others left behind and now I must learn a new job. I had to evaluate a teacher who was making improvements but got back into the school system after being removed due to not receiving a contract, so now I was being asked to get her out again, but she was truly doing a better job. People were sent to help get the job done but it was something that I had to complete along with running a truly toxic environment. It was like being in a psychiatric ward because several of the students had been institutionalized for brief periods of time. The resources were not there. I could not believe the numbers that were being sent. We were being sent the worst of the worst and was saddened by what I saw. I was being made the scapegoat for an already failed program.

I took one for Christ with no regrets. I tried everything humanly possible with my skill set and pat myself on the back loving children who needed love despite people not caring enough for their safety and well-being. Many children were sent to me and had to fight to survive after being placed in an environment that was toxic because of the severity of other students' issues. I was the building leader and the behavior specialist not because I wanted to, but because I had to. I reported everything and was told I was shooting myself in the foot. No, I was doing what God called me to do. I was hired by man but I was working for God. Finally, I had taken my rightful place. The program was made better because of this, all glory to God!

Growth 101 - One regret I had was listening to my boss about evaluating teachers who truly were growing and what I did to her came right back to me. I say remember who your real boss is. LESSON LEARNED!

My job had always been to assist teachers, but sometimes we can make wrong judgements. She should have never been allowed back in the system. I worked awfully hard to bring in support to assist them. My greatest God-given gift is to teach teachers how to be great teachers, and now I had to remove her from a system that failed. Once again help was on the way to assist cleaning up their mess.

I was the new interim center leader of an alternative school which was equivalent to the role of principal, but without the pay and not as much responsibility in some respects. I already had a taste of the publishing world. I was a bestselling award-winning author in a book entitled *Soul Source* for sharing my story of domestic violence. I was a part of a book launch and the book was posted in the Huffington Post. I am traveling the world meeting new people and being celebrated in an arena that overlooked me and now wanted to embrace me. In the beginning, all was going well, and the school was running well, then they started overloading me with the most challenging students I had ever seen. Why would a student be sent to a school when it is known that the program is not equipped? It was like being set up to fail.

The district testing coordinator came on a testing day and he was not happy at the testing site and neither was I. I had untrained staff, was sent the worst cases and when it came to RTI, proper procedures were not followed. I was reprimanded and was trying to fix a program that went from one problem to another. If I just went with the program, maybe my account would have been better. I received a low midterm evaluation and thought "I gave this program everything I had, and this is what I get?" I had never worked so hard in my entire career to help students and had every obstacle possible in my way. I was assuming that I received three ratings of "unsatisfactory" on my evaluation because I was new to the position. My evaluation as a behavior specialist was exemplary. This was before accepting the new position the following school term. I received three ratings of unsatisfactory on my midterm and a few months later, at the end of the year, I received an overall unsatisfactory evaluation for the first time in my career.

I was supposed to be placed on a *Professional Development Plan* (PDP). This overall rating I received was not an accurate reflection of all my hard work this year with the students at this school. A proficient rating would equal a total score of at least 14 to be an overall score of "proficient." I was receiving an unsatisfactory evaluation under Leader Keys Effectiveness System (LKES), but now having to remediate under Teacher Keys Effectiveness System (TKES) because I was now going back in the classroom as a teacher. For me it makes no sense and will never make sense. The system needs to change its rule at the State level, and I doubt if there is anyone fighting for this. For the first time in my career I was in a fight for my job and I also felt targeted. I never worked so hard through my entire career to receive a subpar score. I personally did the district a favor to take the position.

On May 14, 2019, I was called to the office and given my annual evaluation. My overall score was so low it was reported to the Georgia Professional Standards Commission which meant that my teaching certification was in jeopardy. I pleaded my case to my boss detailing the true nature of the challenge that I faced in that position:

- This had been my first year as an administrator for which I had no prior training.

- I was moved from a behavior teacher to a center leader.

- 3 of my teachers were either new to the district or new to the public school system.

- A retired teacher was assigned to split a classroom due to behavior issues and numbers.

- Two teachers were struggling with classroom management and one was on PDP.

- The other teacher was a new hire recommended to continue to work on classroom management.

- We had several substitutes throughout the school year.

- The former schools needed to hold manifestation determination (Follow RTI transfer procedures outlined by the manual) and meet with the school to assist with progress monitoring, many students were sent just before testing which created issues.

- My testing coordinator was changed due to lack of Georgia Milestone Assessment System (GMAS) training and I had to use my guidance counselor (who could have assisted with student behaviors) as the testing coordinator.

During this time of turmoil, God gave me a glimpse of what was to come and revealed that I would be able to retire after twenty-eight years with full benefits. I saw demonic forces in operation. My boss would give me specific instructions and then deny that she did. I had never worked with anyone in authority that I could not get along with, so this was difficult for me to navigate. My boss was facing pressure because a light was being shed on a failing program. I was tasked to complete the duties and responsibilities of others so that they would not be exposed as ineffective. While in this position, my life was out of balance and I barely had time to eat, or drink a glass of water. The day-to-day stress of the job was tremendous. I was burned out and felt I had no other options. I knew there were worse things happening behind the scene that were not being reported in other schools. I, on the other hand, reported everything that happened, and I was told by my immediate supervisor that I was exposing myself. I was not ready for a position that required cover ups and did not want to be in a position that required me to be dishonest because God was requiring me to live a life of transparency.

I remember sitting in my first principals meeting in awe of being there but also remember the conversation in my supervisors' car and being told not to breathe a word about getting promoted.

I felt like I was being bribed to take the position and although I deserved the position, I realized that it was not man that promoted me, but it was God and I believe He placed me there to expose the program. While I was still at the high school, He told me during a spiritual encounter that I would have to take legal action before retiring and when I received the worse evaluation ever, I thank God for the strength to standup despite the outcome. I left this position with my dignity and respect.

The more difficult matters became, the more I learned to trust God, remain pleasant and pray for those who were being used to persecute me. My trust for man was shaken. Proverbs 3:5-6 NIV, "Trust in the Lord with all thine heart, and lean not unto your own understanding. In all your ways acknowledge him, and he will make straight your paths." God was a better judge of what is best for me and I had to trust him in every choice I made. For many years my voice was silent due to the domestic violence that I had endured throughout my life, but when God gave me my voice back, I knew I had a voice and people listened. I had to learn when to speak and when to guard my tongue. Proverbs 21:23 (KJV), "Whosoever keepeth his mouth keepeth his soul from troubles." It is hard sometimes to admit your own faults, but when you see it for what it is you become a better person. God made it plain that I was working for Him and He is my real boss. The bottom line was, I knew I was growing in a different direction and wanted more for my life and God allowed me to stand up for what was right in his eyes and that is all that matters.

Disheartened at the way I was being treated after 27 years of service I wrote a detailed letter about my concerns. Before I left that job location, I prayed over the office, the new principal's office, and every classroom. When I walked out the door, I knew my job was done and despite all the hell I had to endure in that building, I thanked God for choosing me as his willing vessel. I learned I did not need a thank you from man because God was going to reward His servant. My time and purpose would be fulfilled in education soon. God had to show me that this was a part of the plan and they were not supposed to see my value.

My crucifixion was plotted and all the people were in position. I was given my final assignment and when I walked into my new setting, I had a sense that it was a set up to not only fail me, but to fail the students as well. By this time, I was numb to this system and was just doing as I was told. The plan was to get rid of me, so I was happy to have a position and even though I was supposed to be placed on PDP (Professional Development Plan) due to receiving a low score at the previous school. I never lost sight of my purpose to impact the lives of students and teachers. Through my last two assignments, I learned a lot of lessons and I learned about how the system worked. I was under constant scrutiny at my new school, I was given the worst evaluation which, once again, prompted the wrath of my executive director who constantly forgot what she had instructed me to do. This turned out to be a blessing in disguise. I hold no anger or animosity but I do know that many teachers and administrators have left before their 30 year tenure due to being bullied out of the school system. I speak for those teachers today and I say thank you for your many years of dedication. Even at the end of my career and through my own persecution, I continued to grow in faith and continued to be a teacher's advocate. Hebrew 11:1 (KJV), Tells us "Now faith is the substance of things hoped for, the evidence of things not seen." God had shown me a bright future.

Growth 101 - I had to have faith no matter what it looked like.

God reassured me during the process that he had my back and as I stepped out in faith he would provide for me. I had to have confidence and believe in God's character, knowing that He is who He says He is. I endured in spite of what was thrown at me, took the punches and continued to trust God no matter what. I may have not passed man's test, but I passed God's test.

My dreams and aspirations always dealt with being in the public eye. I wanted to be a model and a singer when I was younger, but what God had for me would be so much bigger and different. Never in a million years did I think that I would be led to ministry because I felt I was not living a life that I saw as befitting to my heavenly Father, but he saw me differently.

Even the worst of the worst teachers don't receive five unsatisfactory ratings on an evaluation, but in my final persecution that is exactly what I received! I could not believe it! I was extremely valuable to the school system, and they knew it would take an army to bring me down so an army was brought in daily. I had never seen so many people come in one classroom to evaluate me in all my career!

At what would be the start of my Spring break and having received what was supposed to be my final persecution, March 1, 2020, I lost my momma, and this date would be engraved in my memory for the rest of my life. It was the first Sunday and I was getting dressed for church. I was looking forward to hearing my Pastor, Alan Dwayne O'Neal, bring forth the word. I was looking for my shoes when the phone rang. It was my daughter telling me to get to my momma's house. "Get here! Grandma is on the floor unresponsive," exclaimed my daughter. They were trying to resuscitate my momma and I was taking more time than I typically would getting dressed because I knew I couldn't handle this. When I made it to the end of the Truman Parkway, two minutes away from my momma's home, I called my daughter and asked about my momma. She said, "momma is gone." I rushed to the house and there was my strong, beautiful, beloved momma on the floor in the hallway. I was stopped by family members and EMS when I tried to rush to her aid and at that moment, I didn't care who was there, my first reaction was to get to my momma. She was not a person who enjoyed hugging and kissing or receiving a lot of affection so for the first time I was able to love on my momma on my terms. My momma was the only constant and consistent human being in my life who never let me down.

I remember praying and talking to her and I felt she heard me. I thought she was coming back, but no, she was indeed gone to sing with the angels. I began having flash backs in my mind of my momma preparing me for her death several months earlier. She told me several times she wanted me to preach her sermon. Little did I know God was preparing me for my momma's death and building me up for another real fight with grief.

I saw my momma's health declining right before my eyes. She would not talk a lot about her health so there were only speculations. A few weeks prior to her death she went to the emergency room with an upper respiratory and bronchial infection but was told she could recover at home. This was the final straw as far as preparing me to exit the school system. I always told my momma, if she became ill, I was going to retire. Life is too short, my momma was gone, and I felt that I could do whatever I chose to do. I was able to use funds from my IRA Roth account to purchase a year back and with my 28 years of service, 7 months of sick leave, and three additional months, I had exactly 30 creditable years of service and was able to retire. My momma would be extremely proud of me. I remember having a vision about two weeks prior where I saw my brother, who had already passed away and in the vision, he said "Dina, I am coming for momma". I just looked in the mirror and said, "Leonard don't start." He laughed and I knew that meant he was coming for her.

I was already tired of the job and had been looking for a way out and God had told me that I would be able to retire with twenty-eight years. He made it very plain, but I did not understand how. After the first book project I had weaved a web of bills. One must understand that in my case there were fees associated with the book project. You must purchase the books to sell, purchase clothes, marketing, and classes to learn the business. There are always vultures out there waiting for you, those who know you are both a hot commodity and a meal ticket for them. You are new to the business because you become hungry for the excitement. In my case, I wanted to help women and enjoyed being in the public eye. My dreams and aspirations always dealt with a much bigger arena. What God had for me would be so much bigger and different. One thing about God, when he chooses you, you will begin the journey of self-discovery and purpose. I could finally put my profession behind me. "For Him, and through him, and to him are all things to whom be glory for forever," (Romans 11:36 [KJV]). Everything depends on God; he deserves all praise glory and honor for his wisdom. Paul ended his discussion on the difficulty of Israel's unbelief by bursting into praise for his Heavenly Father. God's purpose has elements of mystery and incomprehension. He is our soul source, and we could never repay him. I had to learn to balance life, ministry and work while trying to help God's children and educators who were struggling due to being overworked, praying for many who I saw in distress. Working for man the rest of my life on a 9-5 was no longer the plan. I was ready to become spirit led and not man led.

FINAL ANALYSIS/GRAND FINALE

As the curtains began to fall, I saw glimmers of hope in getting closer to the person God called me to be. I saw beacons of light and hope for others who were going through or have been through similar situations in their lives. Through my truth and transparency, someone else will be able to do the same. By looking at patterns in my life and the men in my life the curtains had to fall. No matter what it looked or felt like, I had to relive the painful parts of being in the world and of the world. I had to acknowledge the many times I had been vulnerable and used, and even though it took a while, I look at life differently now. As I peek through the curtain, the view is clearer. I had become tired of meeting unavailable men who were not sure what they wanted. God had to save me from myself and show me He is omniscience, omnipotent, and omnibenevolent. I had to fall to my knees and ask God to show me the right path, point out all the curtains that had to fall. I felt like every time I tried and dated it would be the wrong man. I asked God to lead me, teach me and save me from a vicious cycle of men who, just like me, were lost and looking to soothe their own pain through sex.

Had I listened to my momma's guidance and wisdom as God used her to speak to me, I could have avoided a lot of heartache, but I wanted to be grown before my time and I thought I had all the answers. When the curtain is falling, it does not feel good because it is self-assessment time. Before I could become a woman of God, I had to position myself to prosper and come to an understanding of what my purpose was therefore allowing self to die. When I opened the curtain I saw a broken, battered, bruised, misused woman who had to let the curtains of bitterness, hatred, unforgiveness, judgement, frustration, denial, and victimization in and decided to let go and let God. That is when He gently removed what was not right. I needed to open the curtain and see me for me. I was judging others and not looking at myself. God does not judge; this is a part of what makes him different from others. Through Jesus Christ we have the power to love one another.

As the curtains fell, I became an ordained minister and preached my trial sermon on February 10, 2019, while in the mist of turmoil. The Time Is Now; There Is Power in Movement was my sermon topic and indeed God was moving me into a greater position in his kingdom. God was continuing to build me and I was learning how to listen for his voice. Waiting with great expectation helped me to rise above all of life's distraction. I began learning patience as I waited. I am a planner; it may not come when you want it, but it will be on time. My first book project gave birth to Finding a Path after Pain LLC which has become a 501©3 nonprofit ministry. The mission of this ministry is to build, create, and empower women and men who have been traumatized due to domestic violence, rape, and incest by providing inspiration, ministering the word of God, praying, counseling, coaching, and mentoring in the area of job training and skills. I will continue expanding my speaking platform based on domestic violence and educating people. I am about women and people empowerment and will continue to allow God to order my steps through coaching, speaking, writing and publishing material.

As the curtain began to fall, I wanted to become less self-centered and more God-centered by learning to give back to my community. I collected donations to assist and improve the lives of women who fell victim to domestic violence. Another passion I have is for the homeless. I spearheaded and created Pack the Purse Homeless Campaign along with Union Skidaway Baptist church under leadership of my Pastor, Alan Dwayne O'Neal Sr. This allowed other churches and organizations to see the need in the community and this initiative gave way to inspire others to start their own campaigns.

Throughout my career and finally in the end, I found meaning in what man called failure and I was able to find lessons and an opportunity to improve and grow. I learned that I was vulnerable at times, but it is important to ask for help early on and connect with those who can support you. I learned how to have a supportive relationship without beating myself up. I learned how to laugh at my failures and use them as an opportunity to grow. I gained a sense of calmness and composure, especially in a difficult situation, and found comfort in stress releasing meditation. I view my pit falls in education from a positive perspective and I am grateful.

I was now able to see what it meant to persevere. Despite, all I went through in my career, I was still standing through the hurt and pain of what would be characterized as failing. I stood tall in the face of all my foes. Perseverance can be described as exhibiting emotional fortitude or reserves and having the ability to withstand adversity. People who have fortitude are described in an admiring way for their courage. The Latin word meaning - Strength. I could persevere in my career. I had a positive start, remained in the race, stayed committed, and I endured to the end. I encouraged myself and through all of the persecutions I could visualize the end.

I learned to watch who I talked to, workplace jealousy is real and people will use you and throw you away. I remember completing an assignment for my boss and during an important meeting, she did not give me credit for it. She was ill prepared and would often say one thing and then forget she said it. I never had a problem with any of my other bosses, so having to constantly defend myself was the ultimate test. God placed me there to expose the program and bring light to the problems it possessed and even though I gave 110 percent throughout my career, to some, it was not good enough and unfortunately, I became the fall guy for a failing program. Many times, the people at the top were not in the trenches and were no longer in touch with the reality. God had to break my heart to heal my heart. I gave so many years to a system that turned its back on me. When God revealed to me that I was growing for his greater, and not my greater, I began to view my job from a different perspective.

When I was demoted back into the classroom, I had no intention of ever working in a leadership position again. I never wanted to lead man's way, so I was in the wrong business. I did not fit in and had to finally realize I was not built to fit in. What was supposed to break me allowed me to believe in myself and finally do what God called me to do. I took a pruning to bring forth much more fruit. God instructed me to leave at twenty- eight years and made sure it was set up so I could. It was time for me to grow and glow. Many great things came out of the mistreatment of me and I thanked God that the weapons formed against me did not prosper. I told God if he got me out of the school system, I would give my life to him and work for his people until the day I died and since I left, God has given me new leadership assignments in his kingdom, Nuggets of Faith prayer call, and Monday Morning Godly inspirations. I am mentoring young women and training others to study and serve the Lord.

The persecution in my career became my resurrection and light for me to share my story. I was a voice for the voiceless teachers who feared retaliation and left the district without speaking up for themselves about the many hardships that they faced.

God allowed me to persevere through what was supposed to break me. A new call required me to form new habits, so I had to believe in myself and set goals to hold myself accountable. Preparation was a crucial component in learning how to build a ministry. I had to study more, research and begin to understand the new world God chose me to now be a part of. I had to seek ministerial advice and guidance from ministers who knew more than I did, and most importantly, I had to seek the guidance of my heavenly father and listen for his voice. This is all new territory, but I am growing and moving in the right direction. My life has purpose because I am walking in my true calling.

Galatian 6:9 (NIV), "Let us not become weary in doing good, for at the proper time we will reap a harvest if we do not give up." I finally realized that perseverance is a vital part of growing in faith and God wants me to persevere no matter what is going on in my life. I must learn to overcome trials, tribulations, the good, and the bad in order to find victory in my Lord and Savior.

I continue to grow in the area of balance in my life. It is like retraining a child how to ride a bike by using training wheels. I had to learn that through difficult times, I had to seek God for the guidance to help me balance my life. I learned to do this through exercise, drinking water, and resting because rest allows healing mentally. I also began journaling to take my mind off the trauma that I had experienced. Meditating and concentrating has assisted me with deeper breathing which often helped with the built-up anxiety and help to calm my nerves due to years of living a stressful life. I had to realize that doing more and being busy was not necessarily helping me cope. I have been finally able to keep a positive attitude despite all the trauma that both my children and I experienced. I

WHEN THE CURTAIN FALLS

had to also realize it takes time and all events in the past, present, and future would bring me to my destiny.

Forgiveness was one of the most powerful things that I could do for those who harmed me and my children and I learned that it is important as Luke 6:37 tells us "forgive and you will be forgiven." Even though I had to learn through the many betrayals to pray for those who hurt me, I also had to admit that I hurt people along the way.

Forgiveness is a gift that God gives us and I had to realize that it was an essential key to my happiness and my new life with Christ. I had to face the fact that I was far from perfect and that many curtains had to fall so that the emotional weight could be released. I prayed that He would release me from all the bitterness and the hurt that I held behind each curtain. I had to forgive the men who violated my daughters and me, and I had to forgive those who persecuted me in my workplace. I had to trust my Heavenly Father through it all and patiently wait for healing which would take place little by little. I knew I wanted to resemble Jesus who is the ultimate example of forgiveness, so I had to yield to the process.

A life of celibacy is the life God told me to live and no matter the sexual desires I may experience, I will continue to do what my Father has instructed. He told me he would grant me a husband, but I had to be obedient and live according to his plan for my life. I knew my life had more meaning than just teaching and that there is, indeed, life after a career. I had to make an impact in my com-

munity by sharing my story of domestic violence in the book entitled *Soul Source*. I had to partner with the director of Safe Shelter
of Savannah by starting an annual drive entitled, "Finding a Path
after Pain". I know firsthand how difficult it is for one to leave
their home with just the clothes on their back. I wanted to be a
bridge over troubled waters because I have travelled through
murky waters.

In furthering my efforts, I created a Facebook community
which consists of men and women from all ethnicities and walks
of life. Whether I am involved in a community effort or sharing my
story, I continue to use my voice to engage people in conversations
about the silent killer with the hopes of reducing domestic violence, molestation, and rape occurrences so that lives may be saved.
My mission is to be a voice for the women and men who have no
voice because they are afraid of judgement and retaliation from the
community at large. I will continue to spread my movement across
the country. Without the book *Soul Source*, I would have never
known that my roots stretched that deep.

I thought my life was ending when these events occurred in
my life, but I found out the day I faced them was the day my life
began. I had to have faith in myself knowing that God was with
me every step of the way on this journey of healing from the pains
of molestation, rape, domestic violence. He knows your inner and
outer hurts, but I had to allow myself to heal from the pain of it
all. I had to let the curtains fall as I had to take a painful trip down
memory lane and walk the red carpet of shame instead of fame. I

finally gave myself permission to grieve over a normal life and relationships. I wanted to heal from what broke me, love no matter the offense, allow others the chance to show me that I could love again and be loved. The abuse has finally ended and my life has finally begun. My momma and brother were now gone, and as the torch was passed to me, I had to pray no matter how I was feeling. I am allowing my testimony to be heard across the world as an example to others that it is okay to let the curtains fall. Abuse is much like the curtain. Instead of running away from what hurt you, run to it by facing it and mending all the broken pieces of your life so you can be whole again. I had to get to the root causes of the abuse so I could make it to the finish line, the everlasting salvation with Christ.

Through my self-discovery journey and deep-reflection I learned that God is always working. I just need to let him do his job. I had to learn to be confident in my abilities in whatever I did. I had to believe that if I dreamed of being an Author since I was a little girl that God would bring it to fruition. I had to realign my life with the will of Christ. Being confident of this, that he who began a good work in me would carry it out until the completion. It started manifesting, but never did I think my dream would become a reality. I can remember being in an exceptional children's workshop and we played a game where we had to write one thing about ourselves that no one would know.

When the time came to discuss the various responses that we wrote. The word author was spoken, and several teachers thought it was me. Look at God. He began to prepare me and give me a glimpse of this world by being a co-author sharing a chapter about domestic violence, but I knew there was so much more to my life that I was unable to tell in that one chapter. God had to continue shaping and molding me because I was not ready after the first book launch to reveal all just yet. It was mind blowing, I went from being a Savannah city girl to knowing and having my name mentioned in rooms across the country. This was awesome because I had been violated by so many women in my life and then I found myself doing the same thing. I began dating men who were unavailable. Never thought about what I was doing. Most of the men were in a relationship, whether I knew about it or not, but bottom line is I violated other people in relationships. I started being convicted more and more as I grew as a woman of God. You must walk different and respond differently as a woman of God. "Therefore if any man be in Christ Jesus, he is a new creature: old things are passed away; behold, all things are become new" (II Corinthians 5:17 [KJV])

Becoming a woman of God means protecting your ear gates from things that are not godly whether it be music, television, or conversation with a man or woman. The goal was to be more like Christ. I had to develop His characteristic through prayer and allowing self to die. I had to open the curtains of my life by looking at new ways to move past the pain of so many failed relationships while thanking God for hiding my true potential from man so that I would not be mishandled anymore. He was shaping and molding me so I could be a living testimony as to what he can do. He performed the miraculous in my career in that I was able to make it to 30 years. It was time to reward a faithful servant. I had to be demoted to be promoted in God's kingdom. He brought me full circle to where my roots began -- in the classroom with small children.

Sometimes it is important to be brought full circle so you can see what it is like to be at the bottom again. God wants to use a humble spirit, someone who can get in the trenches for his people. It was already ordained that I would be persecuted in man's world, but what man did not realize is that I was under God's protective covering and the curtain would fall for all men to see. All the failed and severed relationships were worth every bit of pain that I may have experienced. I had experienced domestic violence, betrayal, rape, molestation, molestation of my daughters, but both my children and I survived what was supposed to make me lose my mind. I had to learn how to be patient and rebuild my life. I am right where God wants me, I do not have to rush the processes of life.

I continue to grow as a Christian woman through reading Christian books on a regular basis and studying the word of God. I just want to be closer to God in any way possible. I asked the Holy Spirit to help me understand what I was reading and prayed for the desires of my heart. I was not sure why I was moving in this direction, but as I continued on the path, God began chipping away at some of my pain. I thought I had forgiven everyone, but I had not. He allowed me to learn more about forgiveness through starting Nuggets of Faith prayer call which focuses on many topics and one topic is forgiveness and how it harms us when we do not forgive. I am also a certified forgiveness and renewal Coach. Going through the certification process allowed me to see the areas of my life that still needed growth.

Psalms 5:10 (KJV) says, "Destroy thou them, O God; let them fall by their own counsels; cast them out in the multitude of their transgressions; for they have rebelled against thee." I was much like David when his enemies lied about him, he prayed, and he knew that God's love would not only comfort and shield him. It was only the breastplate of the Lord that kept him here. I had to remember that God's love out weighted the evil forces in my life. God was indeed holding me together even when things were falling apart. I didn't know at the time that through my momma's prayers and God's provision of the Spirit of Jesus Christ that what happened to me would become my deliverance and testimony one day.

I eagerly expect and hope that I will in no way be ashamed but will have sufficient courage. "For I know that as you pray for me and the Spirit of Jesus Christ helps me, this will lead to my deliverance." (Philippians 1:19 [NLT]) "According to my earnest expectation and my hope, that in nothing shall I be put to shame, but that with all boldness, as always, so now also Christ shall be magnified in my body, whether in life, or death" (Philippians 1:20 [ASV]). Just as this was not Paul's final imprisonment in Rome just like Paul awaited his trial knowing he could either be released or executed, I too had to trust God despite everything that had happened in my life. Sometimes all the curtains must fall. I had to revisit the color scheme of my life so I could begin to rebuild a new life by adding a new fabric which would lead to beneficial relationships, forgiveness, and balance.

There are so many things that can destroy or damage the fabric of a curtain. My life was much like a curtain and I had to make sure my new foundation was built on Jesus Christ. I had to let all the curtains fall, so that God could place a long-lasting durable fabric on all the windows when he was starting to mold me into his magnificent tapestry. Like Ester, God was working behind the scenes. There was a divine purpose like when God was arranging the many secular events to save the Jews. God was doing the same for me. Sometimes relationships must be severed so that one can move forward in God's grace. I had many relationships that needed disconnection. I was still looking for a relationship with an earthly man, but God was the be all and do all. I needed balance in my life and relationship overhauls. God was trying to realign my life and what I thought were storms was simply the sunshine trying to peak through. I had to let all the curtains fall by allowing God to become my number one priority.

I am now a woman of God. He ordained me and I must walk as I am supposed to. Without balance, the foundation is not solid and I fought for many years to find balance in my life. Anyone can go back and make a brand-new start; anyone can start from now and make a brand new ending. I wanted to live again, thrive again, and use my God given gifts and talents.

Finally, sometimes death must take place for someone else to give birth and both times God was birthing me. I had to lose in so many areas of my life. I had to hear and move; you see a shift must take place. Now the grand finale can begin, I thank God for my Exodus, yes life had to be taken so that I could now walk in God's full anointing power. I thank my Heavenly Father for the gifts transferred from both my momma and brother to me.

ABOUT THE AUTHOR

Redina Maria Thorpe Thomas

Redina Maria Thorpe Thomas is a bestselling author, Renewal and Forgiveness Coach, ordained minister, and domestic violence advocate.

A proud alumnae of St. Vincent's Academy of Savannah Georgia, Redina holds a Bachelor of Arts in English and a Master's in Education and Leadership. Newly retired after serving for over 30 years as an educator, Redina has given back to her former high school by serving as a chairman for the school board. She is a two-time Teacher of the Year nominee, Special Education Teacher of the Year nominee, and member of Phi Lambda International Honor Society.

As a champion of women's rights, Redina is the Founder and CEO of Finding a Path After Pain Ministries and is a domestic violence advocate who has shared her story on numerous platforms across the country. She tirelessly coordinated domestic violence and homeless campaigns in her hometown to assist with distributing necessities to those in need, as well as helping to provide financial and spiritual support. She strongly believes that our gifts and talents are to be used to bring God glory and honor, and it is crucial that all people find their God given purpose so that they can become agents of change in God's kingdom.

Redina is also the Founder of Nuggets of Faith Prayer Call, Monday Morning Godly Inspiration, and Finding a Path After Pain online Facebook communities. Her Facebook group and business logo were inspired by God after she found her path after pain. As a Renewal and Forgiveness Coach, she takes pride in any task that she performs and will go the extra mile to obtain success for her clients.

Redina decided to embark on new projects after being asked by an accomplished author, Cheryl Polote Williamson, to be a part of a Christian women's anthology which allowed her to begin healing from the wounds of her past. Education was her first vehicle, but finding God is the real reason she can do His will for His people. As a bestselling award-winning author for the book Soul Source, Redina served as a proud co-author of the book nominated as an Indie Author Awards Finalist and was a recipient of the 2017 Soar Award.

A mother of three adult daughters and grandmother of three grandchildren, whom she adores, this formerly shy Catholic schoolgirl who found her voice later in life currently resides in Savannah, Georgia.

www.ingramcontent.com/pod-product-compliance
Lightning Source LLC
Chambersburg PA
CBHW071825090426
42737CB00012B/2186